S

NATURE WALKS

AROUND
VANCOUVER

GREYSTONE BOOKS

Douglas & McIntyre
VANCOUVER/TORONTO

00 01 5 4 3 2

Greystone Books
A division of Douglas & McIntyre Ltd.
2323 Quebec Street, Suite 201
Vancouver, British Columbia V5T 4S7

Canadian Cataloguing in Publication Data

Cousins, Jean, 1928 –
    Nature walks around Vancouver

ISBN 1-55054-562-0

    1. Nature trails—British Columbia—Vancouver Metropolitan Area—
Guidebooks. 2. Natural history—British Columbia—Vancouver
Metropolitan Area—Guidebooks. 3. Vancouver Metropolitan Area (B.C.)—
Guidebooks. I. Title.
QH106.2.B7C68 1997   917.11'33044   C96-910831-1

Editing by Barbara Pulling
Cover and text design by Peter Cocking
Cover photography by Tim Matheson, Trudy Woocock's Image Network
Typesetting by Rhonda Ganz & Peter Cocking
Printed and bound in Canada by Transcontinental Printing
Printed on acid-free paper∞

The publisher gratefully acknowledges the assistance of the Canada Council and of the British Columbia Ministry of Tourism, Small Business and Culture. The publisher also acknowledges the financial support of the Government of Canada through the Book Publishing Industry Development Program (BPIDP) for its publishing activities.

Contents

Introduction

This book describes thirty-five walks in and around Vancouver, and tells something of the plants, birds and animals that might be seen along the way. It is intended for anyone who can walk a trail, however slowly, and for those who have never tried.

These walks, which are arranged geographically, have been selected from the various natural habitats of this region, exploring forest and mountains, rivers, fields, beaches, lakes and wetlands. They range from Squamish in the north to Aldergrove in the south, and eastward towards Mission. All are within 65 km (40 miles) of Vancouver, and several are only minutes from the city centre, by car or bus. For the walks that are farther afield, directions for getting to the trailhead should be followed in conjunction with a map of Vancouver and environs. Bus routes are mentioned only when they go to the trailhead, or very close to it, and should be checked with B.C. Transit at 521-0400.

Most of the walks are flat, several smooth enough for wheelchairs and strollers. Other trails have ups and downs and a few are rough underfoot, but all are suitable for families and can be walked in less than two hours. They range in length from 1 km (½ mile) to 7.5 km (4½ miles), the approximate round-trip distance being given in kilometres and miles at the beginning of each walk. All the walks have been surveyed within the year prior to printing of this edition, and the descriptions reflect conditions at that time. However, even well-established trails, and the roads leading to trailheads, can suffer alteration, so be alert to possible changes in route.

Nature Walks around Vancouver is about walking for discovery and appreciation—the first steps towards understanding and preserving nature where we live. Today we are fortunate to have many park and wilderness areas around Vancouver, supporting abundant plant and animal life, but land-use pressures are increasing, and unless we value and protect what we still have, natural habitats will be eroded and our environment degraded beyond hope. One of the best ways to add our voices to the debate on how to use the land is to be part of a group such as a local natural history society. To find out more about these, contact the Federation of British Columbia Naturalists at 321 – 1367 West Broadway, Vancouver v6H 4A9 (604-737-3057).

Some Notes on the Region

The region around Vancouver is divided into two distinct geographical areas: the Coast Mountains and the Fraser Valley, or Lowland.

The mountains of the North Shore, which form a striking backdrop to the city, are the southern end of a range extending 1700 km (1020 miles) north from Vancouver to the Yukon. Locally, they are forested with western hemlock, western red cedar and Douglas fir. Numerous rivers and creeks have carved canyons down their slopes, and large freshwater lakes lie among their folds. Walks such as Cedars Mill Trail, Goldie and Flower Lakes, Yew Lake and the Giant Fir Trail venture into this environment at subalpine and lower elevation.

To the east and south of Vancouver lies the Fraser Valley, through which the Fraser River, widening after the constrictions of the Cariboo and Hell's Gate canyons, swallows up the waters of the Pitt, Coquitlam and Brunette rivers and thrusts its way against incoming tides to the sea. From the Houston Trail near Fort Langley you can digress to view a wide sweep of the river. Both Deas Island and Fraser River parks offer riverside walks. The gently rolling farmland and mixed forest of the floodplain can be explored as you follow the course of lesser creeks on the Campbell River, Pepin Brook and Serpentine River trails.

As the Fraser nears the end of its 1378-km (850-mile) journey, it divides into two main arms, the northern one branching yet again before it reaches the ocean. A wide delta, stretching from New Westminster into the Strait of Georgia, provides rich agricultural land and bountiful habitats for fish and birds. Walks along Blackie Spit, Boundary Bay dykes, Sturgeon Bank marshes and the Reifel Bird Sanctuary on Westham Island afford a wonderful opportunity to see the millions of transient and wintering waterfowl that frequent the fields, mudflats and marshes of the delta. In the Delta Nature Reserve you can walk along the fringe of the largest raised peat bog on the west coast of the Americas.

Vancouver's shoreline is varied, ranging from the sand and shell beaches of English Bay and the mudflats of Burrard Inlet to the rocky headlands of Lighthouse Park and the pebble beach at Porteau Cove on Howe Sound, each environment supporting its own communities of intertidal and marine life.

The Art of Nature Walking

Today, through our computers, we can find instant, expert information on any subject that interests us. But how can a spoon-feeding of facts be compared with knowledge gained from experience? What better way could there be of learning about nature than first-hand appreciation—getting out there and looking?

A nature walk is sometimes an organized outing undertaken in the company of an experienced naturalist. Or it can be a self-guided walk, where the route is furnished at strategic spots with informative panels. These experiences can be enjoyable and worthwhile. But even more satisfying is a walker's own journey of discovery, undertaken for the pleasure of observing the character of the ground trodden and the plants and creatures encountered.

We do not have to go far afield; a half-mile walk can be rich in interest if the walker is trying to understand the natural history of that half-mile. Within our city are pockets of wilderness where we can see eight-hundred-year-old trees; beaches where we can find shells and intertidal creatures. Our coastal marshes attract millions of migratory waterfowl and shorebirds; the mountains on the north shore of Burrard Inlet are laced with wilderness and subalpine trails, many within the ability of even a modest walker. Some city parks are oases for ducks and songbirds, and a neighbourhood ravine can shelter small creatures among its trees and shrubs.

Even if we take the same walk every day, there will be something of interest to meet the observant eye. The nature walker knows where to find yellow violets along the familiar route, when to look for the first salmonberries, which bush conceals the towhee's nest. As naturalist John Burroughs says, "To learn something new, take the path today that you took yesterday."

For some, it will be enough simply to observe things. For others, the identification of their discoveries adds greatly to the pleasure. For them, a good local pocket guide is in order. Don't hesitate, either, to call a park naturalist for advice—they are invariably helpful and can share local knowledge not found in books.

Latin is recognized throughout the world as the language of science. The system of classification developed by Swedish naturalist Carl von

Linné more than two centuries ago divides the animal, vegetable and mineral kingdoms into classes, orders, genera, species and varieties. The Linnaean system, as it is called, was brilliantly conceived and is still used today as a tool for identification. But those who turn to scientific sources of information need not be put off by unfamiliar botanical names. Almost all plants, birds and animals have common names, often several, depending on locality.

HOW TO SEE MORE

Knowing what to look for and how to look for it comes with experience, but a few tips may help to increase your enjoyment of nature walking.

When you take a walk, train yourself to see more than the general view. Take a close look at things. Be quiet. Listen. Take a photograph if you like, but you will learn more if you let your eye be the camera. A sketch is a better idea, no matter how inexpert, because drawing requires looking at the subject carefully. In time, you might want to keep a notebook in which to record your discoveries. But first, establish the habit of looking.

Learn to read signs: tracks in snow and mud, runways through vegetation, tunnels in snow all tell of the comings and goings of wildlife. An overturned stone or log, a nipped twig, scattered feathers, stores of cones and seeds are signs of feeding. Wild creatures' homes and resting places are not difficult to spot—nests and burrows, a hole in a tree, matted-down vegetation.

Get to know a plant or animal's needs. Every organism has a preferred home base, or habitat, that provides it with food, water, space and shelter. When you know an organism's needs, then you know what you might expect to find in a certain habitat, and oddly, if you know what to look for, you are more likely to see it.

If you think you see or hear something, stop and wait; birds and animals will stay hidden until they think it is safe to move. And practise looking at things out of the corner of your eye; a head-on stare signals aggression to most wild creatures. A foraging bird or animal will often let you get close if you walk slowly past without turning your face towards it.

Walk at different times and in different weather conditions. Most animals are active in the early morning and at twilight, and that is a good time to observe them. Frogs, toads and salamanders are often abroad during showers, as are birds, who come down to bathe in the puddles.

Learn to recognize bird calls. There are territorial songs and courtship songs; alarm calls and squawks of aggression; family talk and the small signalling cheeps of a feeding flock.

A final plea: respect all plants, animals and habitats. Don't be tempted to take specimens. If you turn over a rock to see what lives underneath, do so gently and replace it afterwards without crushing to death those whose home it is. Stay on the trails. Pack out your litter and leave the countryside unspoiled for others to enjoy.

WHAT TO TAKE

Walking shoes are adequate for almost all the walks in this book, but light hiking boots might be preferred when trails are wet and muddy. Otherwise, no special clothing is needed, so long as you are comfortable and warm and have some protection from the elements.

A knapsack is not necessary unless you are planning to picnic, but plenty of pockets are a boon. In them you can carry your trail guide, plant and bird identification books, notebook and pencil, and a hand lens for examining mosses or insects. Binoculars are indispensable for observing birds. A magnification of 7 x 35 or 8 x 40 is considered ideal.

And do take along some children if you can. A child will point out things you might never have noticed, dulled and preoccupied as you may be with worldly matters. By encouraging children to join you on nature walks, you could be bequeathing them a lifelong joy and interest—and our future environment will be safer in their keeping.

SAFETY

The most likely hazard you will encounter on these walks is the wooden bridge or boardwalk made slippery by the damp. You can't be too careful where these are concerned.

On some of the walks there are steep cliffs and swift-flowing creeks and rivers; take extra care of children around these features.

Seeing a bear is a memorable experience, but remember that bears are unpredictable and potentially dangerous. Do not approach or attempt to feed one. Avoid surprising a bear by making your presence known—talk or sing when you are in bear country, or tie a bell to your pack. Learn about bears from the bear safety guide supplied to the parks by the Province of B.C. Wildlife Branch.

There is little chance of anyone getting seriously lost on the walks in this book. Trail markers, along with my map and trail descriptions, should be enough to keep a walker on course. Still, it is wise to be aware of some basic wilderness rules:

- Before you set out, tell someone where you plan to go.

- Choose a fine day for a mountain walk, and if the weather deteriorates, do not hesitate to abandon the walk. Give yourself plenty of time to complete the route within daylight hours.

- If you lose sight of trail markers, go back to the last one you saw and start again. On subalpine outings, you could take along the recommended essentials for hikers: food, water, extra clothing, compass and topographical map, pocketknife, flashlight, matches and first-aid kit.

- If you do become lost or you are exhausted or injured, it is best to stay where you are until someone finds you. Don't be tempted to follow a creek downhill, as this may lead you into canyons where you will be hidden from rescuers.

YEAR-ROUND WALKING

Most of the walks in this book can be taken at any time of year, and a delightful bonus for the naturalist in our temperate region is the constant change imposed by the seasons upon the natural world. Each season has something marvellous and particular to offer the nature walker.

In March and April, the urge to get outdoors is irresistible for most of us. We are not the only ones on the move then. Many birds that have wintered here are departing for their northern nesting grounds. Others are arriving from the south to spend the summer. Rodents are leaving winter nests and scurrying about for food, making life easier for predators. Newts and toads come out from their leafy blankets and head for the ponds; frogs are already tuning up for the spring chorus. The first trilliums will appear in the woods now; in open places you might spot the tiny scarlet heads of British soldiers, a lichen found on rocks and logs. Yellow violets, red-flowering currant and deep pink salmonberry flowers soon follow, along with the broadleaf maples' hanging green clusters. By the end of April, fragrant crabapple blossom will perfume the air.

May is really the naturalist's month. The last of the summer migrant birds have arrived and there is birdsong all around. Many nests have fledglings. The mammals, too, have young, and there is a better than usual chance to spot them as family demands keep parents on the hunt for food all day long. Woodland trails are lined with wildflowers, and plants are beginning to flower along the edge of the water as well.

Through the month of June, spring merges into summer. Wild roses and Scotch broom take over open spaces; daisies fill the meadows. By the end of this month you will at last be able to explore walking trails at higher elevation, where lupins, Indian paintbrush and false hellebore await you.

By July, the woods are becoming silent as birds go into their summer moult. Heavy summer foliage obscures the scene for the bird-watcher, so this is a good time to walk in the fields, where butterflies are having their day, and snakes are out sunning themselves. By August, blackberries have begun to appear; red elderberry, arbutus and Pacific crabapple are all fruiting now. August is a good time to walk the dykes along the estuarine marshes as the largest waves of shorebirds arrive.

As the days grow shorter in September and October, many birds are departing for warmer regions while other travellers take their place. Ponds, lakes and sloughs are thronged with waterfowl. Most flowering plants bear seedheads now and entrust their treasure to the birds and the wind. While frogs are sinking into the mud at the bottom of the pond, salamanders and toadlets take to the land to search out terrestrial wintering spots.

Decay and change are all around us in November, as vegetation dies and autumnal gales bring down the last leaves and sometimes the trees. But decomposition has no finality in nature, where death implies rebirth. November is the great month for mushrooms. A walk in the forest will reward with the sight of many fascinating fungi, especially after heavy rain. Thousands of snow geese settle in around the Reifel Bird Sanctuary on Westham Island, and a mixed company of ducks dabbles contentedly on ponds everywhere.

If the roads are clear during December or January, you can make a trip to the Brackendale dykes, where hundreds of bald eagles congregate annually to feast on the spawned-out salmon of the Squamish and Cheakamus rivers. It is often possible to walk in the woods in winter, too, and the dykes are also good for winter walking. Coastal marshes and farmlands take on a tundralike appearance; hawks and coyotes watch for any small creature that wanders abroad. Other predators, too, must hunt to survive, and you might spot the tracks of a fox or weasel in the mud or snow, telling the story of chase and capture.

With February comes the thaw, and often the deluge, conditions that might tempt us to stay indoors, but the walker who braves the weather will see more of spring than those who wait for sunny days. There are buds on the branches, alder and hazel catkins, pussy willows; skunk cabbage emerges from the mud, and we are surprised by the early leaves of Indian plum. But most wondrous of all—the birds are singing. Spring is on the way.

Key to Maps

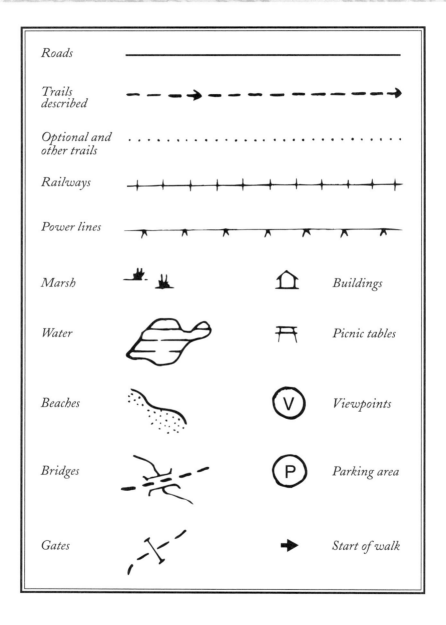

Roads	———————————
Trails described	– – – → – – – – – →
Optional and other trails	· · · · · · · · · · · · · · · · · · ·
Railways	―+―+―+―+―+―+―+―+―
Power lines	―⅄―⅄―⅄―⅄―⅄―

Marsh			Buildings
Water			Picnic tables
Beaches		(V)	Viewpoints
Bridges		(P)	Parking area
Gates		→	Start of walk

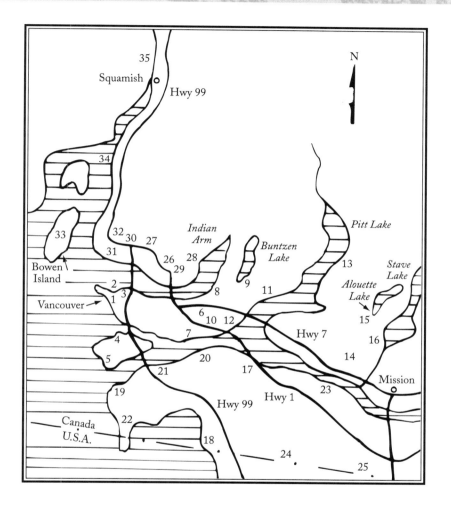

N

35
Squamish
Hwy 99

34

Pitt Lake

33

32 30
27
Indian
Arm
Buntzen
Lake

31
Bowen
Island
26 28
29
13
Stave
Lake

2
8
9
11
Alouette
Lake

Vancouver
1 3
6 10 12
15

7
Hwy 7
16

4
20
14

5
17
23
Mission

21

19
Hwy 99
Hwy 1
24

Canada
U.S.A.
22

18
25

1
Pacific Spirit

PACIFIC SPIRIT REGIONAL PARK
VANCOUVER

HIGHLIGHTS
Coniferous and deciduous forest; dogwoods, aspen, witches' broom;
cedar waxwings, kinglets, grosbeaks

SEASON
All year

ROUND TRIP
2.8 km (1 ¾ miles)

TERRAIN
Flat. Forest trails.

FAMILY WALK
Visit the park centre on 16th Avenue west of Blanca to learn about
events and nature programs for families.

ACCORDING TO HISTORY, the Spanish and British explorers of the
1790s landed on the shore of the peninsula we know as Point Grey, there
to be greeted in friendly fashion by the people of the village of
Musqueam. The Musqueam people still live on their village site, albeit
in a different manner from that of their ancestors. After the explorers
came Simon Fraser, fur trader, followed in 1865 by Colonel Edward
Stamp who built a sawmill, and Jeremiah Rogers who kept it supplied
with timber from the virgin forests of Point Grey. Other lumbermen
followed them, and by the early 1900s only the most inaccessible trees
were left, mostly along the cliffs on the south side of the peninsula. In
1923 the land was endowed to the newly founded University of British
Columbia. Some minor cutting continued until 1945, after which no
more permits were issued, and the forest was left to regenerate in peace.

In 1989 the 765-ha (1900-acre) tract of forest and foreshore was dedicated as parkland. Today, an extensive trail system explores the different
ecological areas of coniferous forest and alder woods, beach and bog.

Sword fern

The park provides a home for small mammals, amphibians, many species of birds and a host of plants. Each form of life establishes itself in its own preferred environment, so that a walk in the park can be a fascinating study.

Originally typical coastal evergreen forest, the region now comprises several different types of habitat, as the effects of logging are played out. Where the land was totally cleared of trees and stumps, alder and birch woods have grown up, with a shrub layer of salmonberry, elderberry and, in drier spots, Oregon grape and salal. Where logging was more selective, the forest grew back more naturally, with deciduous trees such as cottonwoods, broadleaf and vine maples establishing themselves. As these trees provided shade, young conifers were able to get a start, and the next stage in the return to evergreen rainforest was begun. On the east side of the park, a small area of peat bog remains— a relic of glacial activity some 12,000 years ago. Restoration work is currently being done in Camosun Bog to preserve the bog's unique plant life and to save it from the shrinkage begun when adjacent land was drained for development.

The signposted, all-weather route chosen for this short circuit will serve as an introduction to Pacific Spirit's network of trails.

Start by walking up the wide track near the information board on 16th Avenue until you see Top Trail signposted on the left at the northeast corner of the reservoir. This is your route. The trail heads southward along a ridge, among western white birches and salal. In early summer, you might spot the handsome white flowers of the dogwood in the forest clearings. In its natural habitat the dogwood is a small forest tree, capable of thriving in shade as part of the understorey. To identify it in winter or early spring, look for an irregularly branched tree with dark, greyish bark. The dark green leaves are oval and pointed at the tip, with veins curving parallel to the edge of the leaf. The dogwood flower is actually the cluster of tiny, greenish-white flowers at the centre of the four to six large white bracts which we think of as petals. These modified leaves are designed to set off the insignificant flower for the benefit of insects. Tight clusters of bright red berries form in August or September, blossoms sometimes appearing again at that time. Aboriginal people found many uses for the dogwood: bows and arrows and knitting needles were made out of the hard wood, and dye was produced from the bark, as was a potion for stomach troubles. Today the dogwood, the floral emblem of British Columbia, is a protected tree, and only the birds are allowed to harvest it.

After crossing Huckleberry Trail, you'll begin to find bushes of snowberry and oceanspray bordering the path. Salmonberry eventually takes over as you pass through a low-lying marshy area, the beginning of Musqueam Creek. A little farther along there stands a rare grove of trembling aspen, members of the poplar family once common in the Fraser Valley before the land was cleared for farming. The leaves of the aspen, dark green above, pale underneath, are loosely connected to a flat stalk that allows them to tremble in the lightest breeze. The aspen had

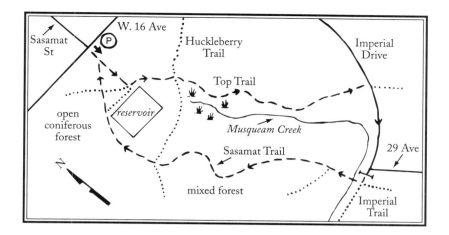

some useful properties for hunters, who discovered that boiling the branches produced a solution good for cleaning their guns and traps. The chalky substance that forms on the bark was observed to be heaviest on the south side of the tree, thus providing an aid to direction-finding. Walkers here will have no need to rely on this, however, since shortly after passing through the aspen grove you will find yourself stepping out onto Imperial Drive.

Turn right on the blacktop and walk along to the bend where it meets 29th Avenue. Beyond the yellow barrier, the road becomes Imperial Trail. A few metres past the park information booth, you'll see Sasamat Trail cutting across the track, a tall dogwood overhanging the trail's entrance to the forest on the south side. Head right (north) on Sasamat for the return leg of your circuit.

First you cross Musqueam Creek, which has taken a sharp change of direction before resuming its southward course. Now you find yourself on a wide, well-used trail, and on fine weekends in any season you will be sharing it with bicycles and dog-walkers. Among the alders and maples stand occasional Douglas firs and hemlocks, trees which were mere saplings during the logging era. Some patches of bitter cherry brighten the way in spring; sword fern and wood fern thrive in the moist, rich soil.

After passing Council Trail on the left, you begin a barely noticeable climb. As the soil becomes drier, the vegetation changes: more conifers are established and salal and Oregon grape reappear, until, after the junction with Huckleberry Trail (you stay on Sasamat), the forest becomes exclusively Douglas fir and hemlock with a canopy so dense that the floor of the forest is bare of vegetation. You may notice that many of the hemlocks along this stretch have odd clumps of branches, known as "witches' broom." This unnatural growth is caused by dwarf mistletoe, a parasitic plant that takes hold beneath the bark and saps the tree's strength. Most of these mistletoe infections occur high up in the tree, but if you could examine one you might see the hairless, segmented stem of the mistletoe emerging from the branch of the tree, bearing tiny scalelike leaves and blueish-green berries. The parasite is common in the park, but appears only to affect the hemlocks. The mistletoe berries are a favourite food of the cedar waxwing, and you might see small flocks of these sleek, crested birds feeding among the hemlocks. Their black masks, yellow tail bands and red wing tips make them easy to identify. These fruit-loving birds have an endearing habit of passing berries from one to another. During courtship, a flower petal might even be presented by a bird to its mate.

Presently you arrive back at the cleared area around the reservoir, bright with the yellow flowers of broom in summer. Follow Sasamat Trail through to its end at 16th Avenue, where your car awaits you—or along which the bus will appear in due course. Pick up a leaflet at the information stand and you will see that there are over 35 km (22 miles) of trails to explore, some of them quite different in character from the circuit you have walked today.

HOW TO GET THERE: Drive west on 16th Avenue to the park entrance opposite the end of Sasamat Street. Park near the information board. Journey time: 15 minutes. By bus: The No. 25 runs west along King Edward and 16th Avenue. Get off at Sasamat.

2
Jericho Park

VANCOUVER

HIGHLIGHTS
Freshwater marsh and ponds, woodland, meadow, foreshore, saltwater bay; ducks, diving birds, shorebirds, gulls and songbirds

SEASON
All year

ROUND TRIP
0.8 km (½ mile)

TERRAIN
Flat. Gravel paths suitable for wheelchairs, forest and meadow trails, lawn and beach.

FAMILY WALK
One of Vancouver's most popular parks for picnics and beach. A food concession is open in summer.

THE DIVERSITY OF NATURAL FEATURES in this relatively small city park on English Bay attracts a wide range of bird life. Migrant waterfowl, shorebirds, raptors and songbirds pass through in spring and fall, adding their numbers to the many birds that regularly nest or feed in the park. Accustomed to human company, resident ducks and songbirds are not shy; even the great blue heron will tolerate an audience.

From Jericho—originally called Jerry's Cove after timber merchant Jeremiah Rogers, who established a logging camp there in the 1860s whilst denuding the region of its giant trees—you can continue walking west to Point Grey or east to Kitsilano. Although trail instructions are hardly necessary for the park, which is spread out before you with the ponds as its centrepiece, I have described a route as a convenient way to mention what you might see as you explore the different environments. Early morning is a good time to visit, when birds are active—a lazy afternoon stroll, on the other hand, might net you a pondfull of dozing ducks and a silent woodland where unseen songbirds are resting on their favourite twigs.

Start from the southwest corner of the parking lot, on the path that stays south of the ponds. Between October and May you might see old squaw, Eurasian and American widgeon, scaup, goldeneyes, green-winged teal and wood ducks around the pond. During March and April a changeover of inhabitants takes place: ducks that have wintered in the park are departing, while others such as cinnamon teal and shovelers are dropping in. Male red-winged blackbirds are arriving to stake out their territory in the cattails in readiness for their mates, who will appear later. By May, mallards will be leading their strings of ducklings beneath the sheltering willows, and coot chicks will pop in and out of the cattail stalks.

What is a park without pigeons? Flocks of rock doves (the proper name for our city pigeons) frequent the little beach at the east end of the pond, where they swirl around the legs of visitors, crisscrossing the sand with footprints. During the summer, southwest British Columbia's wild band-tailed pigeon might also be seen in city parks, especially where there are conifers and berry-producing shrubs. Look for a large, handsome pigeon with yellow bill and feet, a white crescent on the nape of the neck and a pale grey terminal tail band. Unlike the rock dove, which breeds year-round, the band-tailed pigeon nests only in spring, often in a Douglas fir. Nestlings are fed at first on "pigeon milk," a liquid produced in the parent's crop. A likely place to watch for this pigeon would be around the two chokecherry trees at the southwest end of the marsh.

Several kinds of swallows will be feeding over the pond in summer, with a hub of activity around the bridge, where barn swallows build their nests of mud beneath the timbers. From this vantage point you can observe the marshy west end of the pond also, with its enclosing cattails, purple loosestrife and beds of water knotweed. From its roots in the mud, water knotweed sends up long stems topped by elliptical floating leaves and pink flower spikes which in summer cast a rosy blush over the surface of the water. During September and October you might see dowitchers, yellowlegs and western sandpipers probing the mud around the western end of the pond.

Continuing on the main trail south of the pond, you have a chance to watch for woodland birds. The northern flicker and varied thrush winter in the woods, along with fox and golden-crowned sparrows, siskins and juncos. By spring they are joined by vireos, flycatchers and colourful warblers. While many birds are busy building their nests in

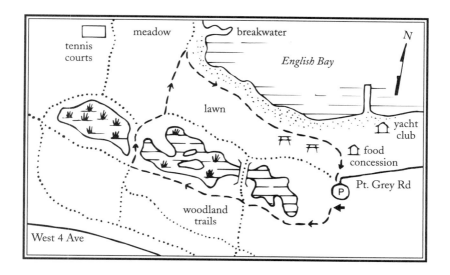

the park, you might see bands of bright yellow and black goldfinches swooping and leapfrogging along in their search for seeds, seemingly without a thought for procreation. Above all else, goldfinches love thistles, and they cleverly time their nesting season to coincide with the thistle seeds in July and August. When it eventually gets down to business, the goldfinch builds a neat cup of tightly woven vegetation, rubbed outside with a caterpillar cocoon to bind it together, and lined with thistle and cattail down. The female incubates the eggs but eschews further housework, apparently content to allow the rim of the nest to become encrusted with excrement as her young hang over the edge to defecate.

If you take the trail between the western end of the pond and the marsh proper, you will see that it connects with a path heading north towards the bay. The scrubby area on the left may harbour pipits and meadowlarks, and is worth exploring along the little paths among the tansy, broom and blackberry bushes. In winter, red-tailed and Cooper's hawks keep an eye on this brushy meadow, where rabbits, mice and voles are tempting prey. Another winter visitor might be the sinister northern shrike, which preys on insects, frogs and rodents, and is not above nabbing a sparrow or chickadee. The shrike waits and watches from its perch, a small grey-and-white-feathered bandit with a black eye-mask and strong hooked bill. To impress the females in their breeding grounds in Yukon and Alaska, the male shrike may hang his prey in the crook of a branch, thus earning the name of butcher bird. Because

Jericho Pond

the shrike has a repertoire of notes and whistles, it is officially classified as a songbird rather than a predator—small comfort to the luckless mouse destined for the butcher's hook.

Finally, you arrive at the ocean, opposite a stone breakwater. Loons, grebes and mergansers all winter in the bay, along with resident cormorants and gulls. In summer our large glaucous-winged gulls are joined by other species, and sometimes by elegant Caspian terns that skim the waves in their search for fish, diving headlong beneath the surface to make a catch. Northwestern crows police the beach at all seasons. Sailboats, freighters, mountains, city, people—there is almost too much to look at as you walk along the sand or make your way back to your transport.

HOW TO GET THERE: From West 4th Avenue, turn north on Alma Street, then west on Point Grey Road. Drive past the Royal Vancouver Yacht Club and Brock House to the parking lot at the end of the road. Journey time: 10 minutes. By bus: Nos. 4 and 42 run along West 4th Avenue, from where you can enter the park.

3
Stanley Park

VANCOUVER

HIGHLIGHTS
Shoreline, forest, lakes, gardens; big trees, oceanspray (ironwood); water lilies; songbirds, waterfowl, shorebirds; raccoons

SEASON
All year

ROUND TRIP
6 km (3 ½ miles)

TERRAIN
Mostly flat, some steps. Seawall, forest trail and garden paths.

FAMILY WALK
There are picnic tables at Ceperley playground and Ferguson Point; a visit to the children's zoo or the aquarium could be included in this walk.

MORE THAN A HUNDRED YEARS AGO, Lord Stanley, Governor General of Canada, dedicated a forested peninsula adjacent to the city "to the use and enjoyment of people of all colours, creeds and customs for all time." There can be few Vancouver residents, or visitors, who do not at some time "go down to the park" to walk, run, cycle, stroll or sit, or to visit the aquarium, the open air theatre, the rose gardens and the restaurants. This walk is a sampling of seawall, forest trails and lakes, with an eye to the plants and wildlife of these different environments. Every season has something to offer: spring and summer for Beaver Lake's songbirds and water lilies, the winter months for waterfowl on Lost Lagoon, and fall for migrating shorebirds along the coast.

From the Ceperley parking lot, walk down through the trees to the seawall and continue northward past the pool at Second Beach. At low tide, green fingers of weed-covered rock point seaward, often occupied by cormorants, gulls or herons waiting to see what delicacies have been uncovered for them. On the landward side, soft sandstone bluffs overshadow the seawall, their crevices supporting tenacious plants and mosses. In June, the creamy white flowers of oceanspray overhang the path, turning later to lacy brown clusters of seed husks that remain on the twigs all winter. Oceanspray is also known as ironwood or arrow wood, because the hard, strong wood was used by coastal First Nations peoples for harpoon and arrow shafts. The wood was heated over a fire to harden it further, then polished with scouring rush. Pegs made from oceanspray were used instead of nails.

Ferguson Point, which you approach next, is a good place to observe winter congregations of diving birds. Thousands of western grebe winter off the point, along with loons, mergansers, surf scoters, buffleheads and Barrow's goldeneye, among others. With binoculars, a local bird-watching guide and a warm coat, you could linger here for hours. The beach itself is fascinating too, made up of an infinite number of broken seashells washed up by the surf. A patient beachcomber, equipped with trowel and hand lens, might find tiny, perfect specimens of bivalves and snail shells.

When you are ready to move on, climb the flight of steps up to the headland and walk across the grass to pick up Lovers' Walk, which enters the forest opposite the restaurant. The trail may not be sign-posted, but a hollow cedar at the start is a good landmark. After you cross Rawlings Trail, which parallels Park Drive, the coastal rainforest closes in around you. Western red cedars and western hemlocks tower above a luxuriant undergrowth of vine maple, huckleberry, sword fern, lady fern and foamflower. The massive stumps left by last century's logging operations have nurtured the seedlings of neighbouring trees and are now straddled and dwarfed by their adopted offspring.

When a snag (a standing dead tree) comes into sight on the left, you are approaching the junction with Tatlow Walk. If there is no signpost, a fire hydrant helps to identify the spot. Cross Tatlow and continue straight ahead through a stand of young Douglas firs planted after the ravages of Typhoon Frieda in 1962. Take the next right fork, and you will soon find yourself on Lake Trail, heading for a safe crossing of Stanley Park causeway via the pedestrian overpass. This brush with civilization over, you descend between ranks of skunk cabbage, turning right at the next junction to join the trail around Beaver Lake.

An anticlockwise circuit works best, but before you set off to the right, take a minute to fine-tune your navigational skills—it is easy to lose track of where you are on this circular trail. Proceed around the marshy south side of the lake amid willows and hardhack, pausing when

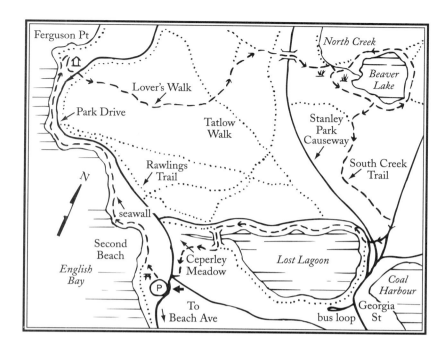

you come to the next trail to the right. Make a mental note of this spot, or make an arrow of sticks or stones here, for eventually this will be your exit point. Now you can carry on with a circuit of the lake, ignoring all right turns until you arrive back at your arrow.

In early summer, water parsley is noticeable among the larger shrubs, often growing with skunk cabbage in standing water. The branching stems bear parsley-like leaves and compact clusters of tiny white flowers. The roots of water parsley were used by Salish people to treat stomach disorders, although it is possible the plant contains toxins similar to those in the poisonous water hemlock. Both plants belong to the carrot family.

Pale marsh violets bloom on either side of the path in spring, followed by a sprinkling of marsh forget-me-nots. On the water side of the path, purple and yellow irises stand guard. A closer examination of the lakeside vegetation might reveal marsh cinquefoil, an aquatic plant, whose striking, reddish-purple flowers secrete a nectar that attracts bees and flies.

The trail opens out to the lakeshore where, in summer, a breathtaking sight awaits you: beyond a fringe of frilly white buckbean, rafts of pink, yellow, white and deep red water lilies cover the surface of the

Beaver Lake

lake. The familiar yellow pond lily, with its floating, cup-shaped flower, is the only one of this aquatic display that is native to British Columbia. Its monstrous rhizomes anchor themselves in the muddy lake bottom, sending up thick, flexible stems and the floating, leathery leaves so convenient for frogs. Water lily roots and rhizomes are still used by Haida people as medicine for various ailments.

As you walk along the shore, mallards and wood ducks push their way between the lily pads to the remaining pools of open water, hoping for a handout. In spring and summer the shrubbery is alive with sparrows, warblers, flycatchers and red-winged blackbirds, while the surrounding forest harbours woodpeckers, brown creepers, nuthatches, vireos and busy flocks of golden-crowned kinglets.

Soon after crossing North Creek and passing your original starting point, you will arrive back at your exit route on the south side of the lake. This trail climbs briefly away from the lake to a junction at which you branch left. Continue southward beneath tall Douglas firs until the rose gardens come into sight. From here, you are nicely placed to walk up through the gardens to the Malkin Bowl or the Pavilion, if you wish, before heading down to cross the causeway via the underpass and joining the path along the north shore of Lost Lagoon.

Canada geese and mute swans can always be seen on the lagoon, along with coots and mallards, a resident population joined in winter by goldeneyes, canvasbacks, ring-necked ducks and flocks of dozing scaup. If you are walking in the park in late June or early July and behold an army of marching geese, you are witnessing one of the roundups conducted by park staff to control the goose population. While incapable of flying during their summer moult, the birds are herded into the tennis courts and loaded into poultry trucks, to be transported to other parts of the lower mainland.

Other Lost Lagoon wildlife you might encounter are skunks and raccoons. Both have become too much accustomed to human company for their own good, and park staff beg us not to feed or try to touch the animals.

In summer especially, a delightful route back to the Ceperley parking lot is to cross the bridge at the west end of the lagoon and walk seawards across Ceperley meadow beside the herbaceous border, where inviting cedar chip paths wind among the shrubs and hostas. The path then heads left alongside the golf pitch-and-putt to end opposite the parking lot. If you are staying out for a picnic around Second Beach, you might like to watch or join in ethnic dancing, which takes place on the Ceperley playground tennis courts on summer evenings.

HOW TO GET THERE: Drive north along Beach Avenue to the Ceperley parking lot on the west side of the park. (The putting green and the Fish House restaurant are opposite.) Journey time: 15 minutes. By bus: Take No. 19 to Stanley Park Loop and walk west along Lost Lagoon to pick up the circuit on the seawall near Ceperley playground.

4
Fraser River Park

VANCOUVER

River and estuarine marsh; river traffic; cattails, snowberries, black-berries; cormorants, red-winged blackbirds; muskrats

SEASON
All year

ROUND TRIP
1.6 km (1 mile)

TERRAIN
Flat. Path, boardwalk and gravel track, some areas suitable for wheelchairs.

FAMILY WALK
This is a popular spot for picnicking, sunbathing and beachcombing, and the park has an interesting interpretive display. Take a pail for blackberries in late summer.

RESCUED FROM THE COMMERCIAL and industrial concerns that dominate the north arm of the Fraser, this unexpected gem of a park provides a needed breathing space in this busy part of the city.

There is a wide grassy area for games and picnicking, seats along the riverbank for watching tugs, barges and log booms, and an outstanding parks display describing the formation of the delta, an account of the Musqueam people who inhabited it, the days of the early settlers, and the growth of the fishing and logging industries at the mouth of the river. The natural history of this remnant of floodplain forest is explained at specific sites throughout the park. A boardwalk affords a unique opportunity to view the estuarine marsh at low or high tide, and to learn something of wetland ecology from both the information panels and on-the-spot observation.

A clockwise, circular walk makes the most of the park, so head east

Cattails

from the parking area, passing the artifact from the Eburne sawmill and a stand of alders and cottonwoods to arrive at the main information display. As you leave the shelter you may notice that a thicket of wild roses and snowberry bushes threatens to engulf the building. Snowberry, also called waxberry, is a member of the honeysuckle family, whose pink flowers give way in August to white, waxy berries, many of which remain on the bare twigs throughout the winter.

As you walk downstream beside the river, there is plenty to look at. Besides the procession of river traffic, gulls, ducks and diving birds are going about their business. In summer the path is bordered by the cheerful yellow blooms of birdsfoot trefoil, growing in a tangle with vetch, loosestrife and spiky dune grasses. Willows have been planted beside the path, but farther ahead, Scotch broom has found its own way here, along with both Himalayan and evergreen blackberries. Though often growing side by side, these two species are easy to distinguish: the evergreen blackberry is the one with deeply divided, raggedly toothed leaves. Both varieties produce delicious fruit, as does our native trailing blackberry—though the latter is known mainly for its scratching and foot-tripping attributes.

Embarking upon the boardwalk you can now observe the marsh at close quarters. Flooded daily by the tides, the largely replanted grasses and sedges of the lower marsh will take many years to reach the maturity of the upper marsh, where cattails, bulrushes, irises and various shrubs provide a habitat for songbirds, herons and small mammals, and for raptors such as owls.

Paths branching off to the right lead onto a kind of island—an area worth exploring. To encourage young fish to stay through the tidal cycles, some standing water has been created by means of a canal. The cattail beds surrounding the most easterly of the bridges over the canal are a feeding ground for muskrats, who feast on the starchy, underground stems. The muskrat is a lively, industrious rodent, equipped for aquatic life with partially webbed hind feet, waterproof fur and even furry lips that close behind its front teeth to facilitate underwater dining. It is equally at home in a burrow in the bank or a lodge built of sticks and vegetation. For this work, the muskrat cuts the cattail stalks into convenient lengths and, after sticking them together with mud, proceeds to munch its way through the centre of the pile until a hollow dome is achieved, and voilà—a nice dry home on the water.

Red-winged blackbirds and marsh wrens also make their nests among the cattail stalks. This useful plant has long been valued by native peoples who ate the shoots, flowers and roots, made flour from the pollen and wove mats from the leaves. Even the fluffy down that extrudes from the brown spikes in fall was used for diapers. Flanking the cattails is another inhabitant of saline and freshwater marshes, Pacific silverweed, most noticeable in early summer when yellow, buttercup-like flowers are dotted amongst the feathery, silver-backed leaves. It too has an edible root, said to taste like parsnips. Away from the water, the island is a wilderness of willow, cottonwood and blackberry bushes, with broom and tansy growing in the open beside the paths.

Although two bridges connect the island with a gravel track on the north side of the park, there is still more to be discovered by returning to the boardwalk. Bulrushes and goldenrod now border the walk, which

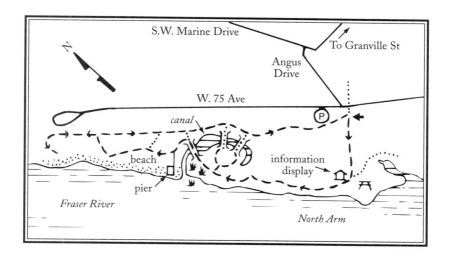

widens into a viewing platform with a bench. Turning left after crossing the bridge spanning the canal, you can stroll to the end of a wooden pier; the beach below is a popular summertime picnicking spot.

Beyond the pier, the boardwalk reverts to a gravel path that cuts through a vast thicket of snowberry, wild roses, salmonberry and thimbleberry. Where the path finally bears right to meet the north-side track, you have a choice. If the tide is low, you can drop down to the beach and pick your way along the sand to the trail's end (where there's a scramble up from the beach) or you can follow the gravel track to the same point. A bench at the turnaround spot is well placed for watching cormorants, either in the water or as they dry their wings atop the nearby pilings.

Returning along the north side of the park—a blackberry picker's paradise in August—you will pass beneath two stands of tall cottonwoods to emerge on the edge of the open field. As you stroll back to your car or bus stop, consider the example of coexistence this small city park affords with its working river and neighbouring industry, its space for people to rest and play, and its thoughtfully preserved habitats for plants and animals.

HOW TO GET THERE: The park is located on West 75th Avenue and can be reached from southwest Marine Drive, just west of Granville Street, by driving south on Angus Drive or Barnard Street. Journey time: 20 minutes. By bus: Take the No. 20 to Granville and 70th Avenue and walk west two blocks to Barnard Street.

5
Sturgeon Bank Marshes

LULU ISLAND
RICHMOND

HIGHLIGHTS
Tidal marsh and rivermouth; Garry Point, Steveston fishing village;
waterfowl, shorebirds, raptors, songbirds

SEASON
All year. Winter best for birding.

ROUND TRIP
5 km (3 miles)

TERRAIN
Flat. Gravel dyke-top, optional informal trail. Garry Point Park paths
suitable for wheelchairs.

FAMILY WALK
Kite flying is a popular pastime in Garry Point Park. There are also picnic tables, a sandy beach and a Japanese garden.

LULU ISLAND, WHICH CONSTITUTES the larger part of Richmond,
lies between the three arms of the Fraser River. Surrounding dykes—
built to control flooding and claim the land for agriculture, and later for
industry and residential property—serve well as footpaths from which
to observe the teeming bird life of the Fraser estuary. Outside the
island's western dyke, the tidal marshes of Sturgeon Bank extend for
several kilometres, providing food and refuge for thousands of resident
and migratory waterfowl and shorebirds. These are brackish marshes (a
mixture of fresh and salt water), increasing yearly as the Fraser continues
to pour its muddy waters into the ocean. On the inland side, sheltered
sloughs and drainage ditches also attract waterfowl, while a few remaining stands of crabapple and cottonwood are a haven for songbirds.

The west dyke extends for 5.5 km (3 ½ miles) from Terra Nova in the
north to Garry Point in the south, with access from the western ends of
River Road, Blundell, Francis, Williams and the Steveston Highway,

Steveston wharf

depending on how long a walk, run or cycle ride you want. Nature lovers might be content with the short stretch suggested, particularly as it includes a possible foray into the marsh itself and a tour of Garry Point Park. Bear in mind, too, that while others are eating up the miles in running shoes or on wheels, you will spend much time standing still, following the flight of a hawk through your binoculars or focussing on a flock of snow geese at the water's edge. Since the winter months are the most rewarding for bird-watching, dress warmly for this outing, and plan on tramping into Steveston at the end (this is included in the distance for the round trip) to warm up with hot soup or some of the town's famous fish and chips.

Among the many ducks you may see from the dyke is the Northern pintail. In January and February it seems that every pool is thronged with these elegant ducks, dabbling and foraging in the icy water and among the sedges. The male pintail has a sleek, grey body, a white neck and a chestnut-brown head, while his mate is equally well dressed in various shades of brown; both are easily recognizable in flight and on the water by their long, spiky tail feathers and long necks.

Scanning farther out over the sea of cattails and bulrushes, your eye might be caught by groups of snow geese flying in from their winter base on Westham Island to feed on the marsh grasses in preparation for the journey back to Wrangel Island in Siberia. Small flocks of tundra and trumpeter swans can also usually be spotted at the far edge of the marsh in winter. Great blue herons stalk and stab in their deadly fashion; the bittern, too, will be poised among the reeds. A bald eagle landing on a branch of driftwood will prompt nearby ducks to fly up and settle at a safer distance. Circling high above the marsh, or skimming the cattails, red-tailed hawks and Northern harriers seek out the furtive movements of mice. Also sharing the rodent bounty is the short-eared owl, often seen flying low over the marsh in daytime. Look for a slender, buff-coloured owl with blackish patches on the undersides of its wings. Its large head and bouncy, erratic flight distinguish it from the harrier, which quarters the marsh with smooth precision.

As you pass the barrier at the south end of the dyke, you will see a sign reading "Nesting Area" and a trail heading west into a belt of trees beside a slough. If you don't mind mud and possibly ice underfoot, you can follow this path for some distance for an on-the-spot look at a tidal marsh. Don't go too far, or wander away from the path, such as it is, because the sedge meadows are laced with channels and change with the ebb and flow of the tides. This path, and another that starts beside the cooperative boatyard at Scotch Pond, are worth exploring in summer as well. Remember they are nesting areas, though, and go quietly.

In summer the scrubby trees and bushes at the start of the trail turn into a glorious tangle of Pacific crabapple, twinberry, hardhack, blackberries and wild roses, with vetch climbing over all. The slough, which was alive with ducks in winter, is now filled with tussocks of marsh grass and bordered by fireweed and cow parsnip, while the meadow to the left

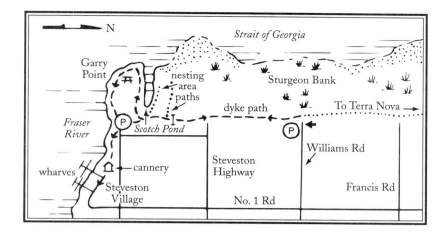

of the trail is bright with irises and loosestrife above a thatch of silver-weed. Here and there, giant dock plants raise aloft thick columns of brown and rose–coloured seeds.

The trail beside Scotch Pond may be impossible to navigate in summer, unless a path has been cut through the blackberry bushes and two-metre-high grass. Even so, you are walking through a tunnel from which you see nothing but stalks. If it is early evening (a recommended time for bird-watching), when the sun is low in the west, you will be dazzled by the glare. But if you stop and simply listen, you'll discover that the air is filled with the calls, whistles, chirps and twittering of birds, as warblers, swallows, sparrows and finches forage for seeds and insects before folding their wings for the night.

Above all, this is blackbird country. Cheerful red-winged blackbirds are common throughout the year, forever proclaiming their territory with a creaky "kon-ka-ree" or seeing off intruders with a peremptory "chack." In spring there is much bowing and flashing of scarlet epaulettes by the males as they set about winning the favours of the modest, brown-streaked females. In due season, a nest of woven vegetation is slung between two cattail stalks, or sometimes in a bush, in which the female settles down to incubate their three to five colourful eggs. The fledglings are fed mainly on insects, but later the family may take to the fields for a diet of weed seeds.

Two other blackbirds can be seen around the south end of the dyke—Brewer's blackbird, the males noticeable for their glossy purple heads and pale yellow eyes; and the smaller brown-headed cowbird, with a short, sparrowlike bill. Flocks of cowbirds frequent grain fields and pastures in the Fraser Valley, where they like to take advantage of the insects that accompany cattle and horses. Ever the opportunist, the cowbird builds no nest of its own, but deposits one of its eggs in the nest of a songbird, leaving the raising of its young to the unsuspecting foster parents, often at the expense of the legitimate brood. Some species, for example robins, recognize the bastard egg as an imposter and toss it out of the nest.

For a change of scene, take a turn around Garry Point Park, from where you can train your binoculars across the Strait of Georgia or watch the river traffic in the busy south arm of the Fraser. Also worth watching are the crying, wheeling gulls that follow the fish boats up the channel, and if you come here in spring when the eulachon are running, you will certainly see seals and California sea lions following the feast.

Steveston is a ten-minute walk away and worth a visit. Hundreds of trollers, gillnetters and seiners are moored in the working harbour and, in season, fish is sold fresh from the boats at the wharf on Bayview Drive. You can choose from a number of restaurants and food stalls, stroll through the craft shops, take a tour of a cannery or visit the museum on Moncton Street and learn about the fortunes of the town since Manoah Steves and his son built a homestead there in 1878.

Eventually it will be time to return along the dyke to Williams Road, a northward journey enhanced on a clear day by views of the Gulf Islands, Point Grey and the north shore mountains.

HOW TO GET THERE: From No. 3 Road in Richmond, turn west on Williams Road and drive to its end at the dyke. Journey time: 25 minutes. By bus: Take the No. 406 from the Richmond Exchange or Granville Street in Vancouver to Williams Road and Seventh Avenue.

6
Burnaby Lake

BURNABY LAKE REGIONAL PARK
BURNABY

HIGHLIGHTS
Lake, marsh, forest; Brunette River; waterfowl, shorebirds, songbirds; squirrels, beavers, muskrats

SEASON
All year

ROUND TRIP
4 km (2½ miles)

TERRAIN
Flat. Cedar chip and gravel trails. The boardwalk at Piper Spit is suitable for wheelchairs.

FAMILY WALK
Children will enjoy the displays and live specimens at the Piper Avenue nature house. There are picnic tables outside.

AS SUMMER DRAWS TO A CLOSE we may feel that for a while nature has nothing new to show us: wildflowers have gone to seed, the leaves have not yet turned colour; the swallows are departing, the wintering ducks have not arrived. And wasps come uninvited to the picnic. It is an in-between time. But there is something to be seen and heard at every season, and a late-August walk along Burnaby Lake trails offers much of interest.

For those who have only glimpsed this green valley from the freeway, the lake is the centrepiece of a 300-ha (750-acre) regional park, the whole miraculously retaining a wilderness character in spite of the proximity of industry, roads and railway. The lake is fed by numerous small creeks and flows into the Brunette River at its eastern end. This outflow is regulated by the Cariboo dam to prevent flooding downstream, also to ensure a steady pressure of water in the lake itself as a safeguard against the slumping of the highway and railway tracks. As the marshy edges of the lake are continually encroaching on the open water, much clearing and dredging is necessary; ongoing arguments with beavers add to the work of park staff in preserving the fragile environment. The hard-won result is a stopping place for migratory birds, almost in the centre of the city, and habitats for songbirds, raptors, waterfowl, fish, frogs and salamanders, beavers, muskrats, raccoons, squirrels and coyotes—and city folk who like to keep in touch with the seasons out of doors. A 10-km (6-mile) trail encircles the lake, part of it shared with equestrians, but for a short nature walk the Brunette Headwaters or Cottonwood trails along the north shore offer the most variety.

With the Piper Avenue spit and viewing tower as a destination, make for the trailhead at the corner of the Avalon parking lot and descend through the woods to the avenue of chestnut trees beside the dam. Crossing the spillway, you stroll beside the Brunette River which, true to its name in colour, moves sulkily towards the dam wall, disturbed only by a plopping frog or floating leaf. The trail swings right, to a bridge over Silver Creek, then continues beneath tall hemlocks and cedars, one of several patches of evergreens in the largely second-growth deciduous forest bordering the lake. Ignore Spruce and Conifer Loop trails for now—this woodland alternative can be your return route—and stay on the Brunette Headwaters Trail as it emerges into the open beside a marsh of sedges and spirea. Tunnels and runways of flattened vegetation mark the regular routes of marsh and woodland creatures.

A common, though rarely seen, inhabitant of the marsh is the secretive Virginia rail. This slender, long-billed bird with a cinnamon breast steps furtively among the reeds in search of seeds, snails and insects. Long toes enable it to walk on top of the vegetation. When disturbed, the rail may fly up awkwardly, long legs dangling, but usually prefers to slip away between the stalks to safety—easy to do when you are "thin as a rail." The sora, the sandhill crane and the less retiring American coot are relatives of the rail.

If you are walking in late summer, you will have noticed by now the abundance of jewelweed, or touch-me-not, plants along the trail. Both the yellow-flowered and the larger pinkish variety seem to be a specialty of Burnaby Lake, often growing together or tangled with other shrubs. The tall annual plants, members of the impatiens family, are named for the way in which their seed capsules explode and fly when the plant is touched.

After passing through a woodland of alder, birch and maple, and finally a row of acacias, you cross a bridge over Eagle Creek to find

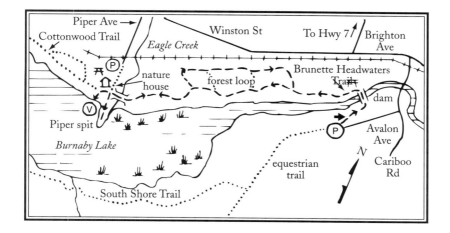

yourself close to the Piper Avenue entrance. To the right is the nature house, open on weekends and holidays from May to Labour Day. Here, park staff are on hand to answer questions, explain the displays and sometimes introduce you to small wild creatures temporarily housed there. Ahead on Cottonwood Trail is a viewing tower; to the left, a blackberry-bordered lane leads to a boardwalk extending along Piper spit. This is the place to go for a close look at the lake and marsh.

Between ranks of irises and purple loosestrife, across beds of water lilies, the boardwalk takes you to a platform overlooking mudflats and stretches of shallow water. By late August you might see groups of long-billed dowitchers diligently probing the mud for worms and crustaceans, putting to shame the flotilla of panhandling ducks and geese that jostle each other around the platform. At most seasons, pintails, buffleheads, green-winged teal, shovelers and mergansers, among others, can be seen on the lake. An evening visit might reward you with the sight of beavers working and playing around their enormous lodge at the end of the spit. For a larger view of the lake and its surroundings, return to the trail and follow the sign to the viewing tower.

If you are not ready to retrace your steps to the Avalon parking lot after sampling the Piper Avenue attractions, you could include a stretch of the Cottonwood Trail in your itinerary, perhaps as far as an open viewpoint about 1 km (½ mile) to the west. You may be surprised to notice hops entwined among the trees along this trail, escaped from a garden, no doubt, and quite eye-catching in September when the pale green cones hang from the vines. The short Piper Mill Loop makes an interesting return to the nature house. This path wanders through an

old mill site where ancient sawdust piles, now sprouting shrubs and fox-gloves, are a favourite playground of Douglas squirrels.

Returning eastward along the Brunette Headwaters Trail, be sure to take in the Conifer Loop. The diversion adds a few extra steps to your walk and takes you through a mix of coniferous and deciduous forest that harbours a variety of birds. Wrens and chickadees, nuthatches, juncos and woodpeckers might all be seen or heard, and in fall, flocks of evening grosbeaks and pine siskins could be foraging in the treetops. At first, the wood-chip trail is carpeted with conifer needles, then some woodpeckered snags on the left mark the beginning of a transitional zone. A number of cascara trees thrive here, content to grow in the shade of the evergreens. Easily mistaken at first glance for alder, the large, dark green cascara leaves are deeply furrowed by almost parallel veins. The bark is smooth and grey. By September, clusters of greenish flowers will have given place to attractive berries in the process of turning from green to purplish-black. Cascara bark has long been harvested for its laxative properties, science eventually confirming what aboriginal peoples have known for centuries.

Many fine Sitka spruce grace the last leg of the forest loop, foamflower and beds of false lily-of-the-valley at their feet. Then you are homeward bound on the main trail, soon to recross Silver Creek and the Brunette River on your way back to Avalon Avenue.

HOW TO GET THERE: From Lougheed Highway (Highway 7) turn south on Brighton Avenue, then east on Winston Street. Turn south to cross the railway tracks onto Cariboo Road, then west on Avalon Avenue at the Burnaby Equestrian Centre sign, and proceed to the parking lot. Journey time: 30 minutes.

FACING PAGE: *Cottonwoods beside Brunette River*

7
Byrne Creek Ravine

BURNABY

HIGHLIGHTS
Forest and creek; Ron McLean Park; shrubs, berries; songbirds

SEASON
All year

ROUND TRIP
4.8 km (3 miles)

TERRAIN
Ups and downs. Forest trail, some steps, park path and road.

FAMILY WALK
Children can look for lampreys in the creek. There are picnic tables and a playground at Ron McLean Park.

ORIGINALLY KNOWN AS WOOLARD'S BROOK, this waterway once flowed eastward through cow pastures and bog. Interference with its peaceful course began in 1893, when a man named Peter Byrne rechannelled the creek to supply a newly dug ditch running through the bog to the Fraser River—an arrangement that allowed the Gilley brothers and other logging companies to float their timber down the ditch to the river and thence to the sawmills in New Westminster. In the 1980s the watercourse was redirected yet again to accommodate road alignment, and today Byrne Creek runs through Riverway golf course on its journey to the Fraser.

The ravine through which this walk wanders has been protected as part of Ron McLean Park and is part of a larger program of saving neighbourhood ravines from development or use as illegal garbage dumps. Although close to Skytrain, flanked by residential streets on the west and apartment towers on the northeast, the ravine remains a belt of wilderness that offers some surprising discoveries to nature lovers. There are several access points from neighbouring streets, including

Salmonberry

Ron McLean Park on Rumble Street, but for a complete circuit the Marine Drive trailhead is the most satisfactory. The westside trail on which you begin was built by the Environmental Youth Corps and includes a fine bridge and a stairway of 185 steps. Don't be put off by this piece of news—the steps are shallow and the whole staircase is beautifully made. The return trail on the east side of the ravine is less formal but still easy walking.

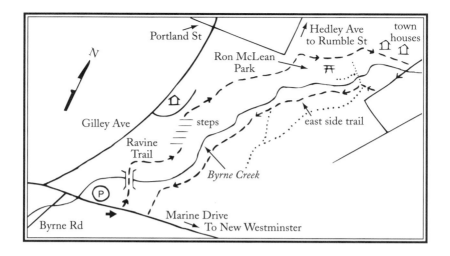

Begin by following the wide track down to the bridge. In spring the creek is quite lively as it fingers its way over the stones and gravel. In June 1995 a group from the Vancouver Natural History Society found lampreys spawning here, at the mouth of the ravine. The society's magazine, *Discovery*, describes them as being about 25 cm (10 inches) long, a group of fifteen swirling about together. Lampreys are parasitic fish which at first glance may be mistaken for eels, but they have a suctorial mouth with which they fasten themselves to their host fish. Scars made by Pacific (sea) lampreys are sometimes found on salmon by commercial fishermen. Those discovered in Byrne Creek were believed to be river lampreys, a species that lives most of its life in the sea, migrating up rivers to lay its eggs in the shallows. Lampreys travelling up a creek would likely have a hard time of it, for they are feeble beings who can only wriggle forward by degrees, frequently clutching at a stone or rock to rest. Hatchlings in the stream feed on microscopic plankton and animals before beginning their parasitic life at sea.

Continuing upstream along the well-made trail, you climb gently through a forest of evergreens, alder and cottonwood, with here and there a surviving old-growth western red cedar. The side of the ravine is hung with sword ferns, and in spring yellow violets and bleeding heart carpet the ground.

Soon you are confronted by the steps. In easy stages, and with several landings from which to admire the view and catch your breath, you climb out of the ravine to emerge beside a street of fine houses. The trail continues through the fringe of trees to Ron McLean Park, where you can rest at the picnic tables while you consider your options for the return leg of the circuit.

If hopping across the creek on rocks holds no terrors for you, head for the northeast corner of the picnic field and descend on the trail, keeping right at the junction, down to the creekside. The place where a large storm drain empties into the creek appears to be the popular crossing spot, from which there is a scramble up the bank and a stiff pull up to the fallen hemlock that lies at the top of the ravine.

If you are not attracted to this idea, there is a more civilized way to circumnavigate Byrne Creek. For this, walk eastward past the washrooms and tennis courts and follow the wide path beyond the posts, townhouses on your left. Turn right when you meet a road, then continue on the track heading south. After a short distance, watch for a trail to the right; the fallen tree mentioned above is visible at the end of it, and that is where you pick up your return route—the right-hand path that follows most closely the edge of the ravine.

Although not marked, this eastside trail is well used and plain to follow. Ignore side trails to the left and steep little paths that descend to the creek. You wind your way along the lip of the ravine among birches and alder, maples and cottonwoods, with a great variety of shrubs beneath them. At most times of year this area is alive with birdsong, the tapping of woodpeckers, and the rustlings and scratchings of ground-foraging towhees.

Sometimes, the very familiarity of our common bushes prevents us from really seeing them, and besides, for part of the year they are nothing but a thicket of bare sticks. Walking here in early spring, you will certainly notice the drooping white blossoms and bright green leaves of Indian plum, brilliant in the still sleeping woods, and perhaps the tiny pink buds of red huckleberry beginning to show. By early April, the salmonberry bushes will be putting forth delicate magenta blooms, and the upright clusters of flowers in the heart of the Oregon grape will be turning from green to a dazzling yellow. Come again in summer and you can take your pick from the fruit of these familiar but marvellous shrubs and plants.

Blackberries need no introduction from anyone, and you will find plenty here. Juicy red or orange salmonberries, guarded by prickles, are ripe by July; in slightly drier spots thimbleberry bushes offer their more seedy fruit, sometimes hidden by the large maplelike leaves but without prickles to catch the foraging hand. Where there is plenty of light, you might find tall, black-raspberry bushes, with their arching branches and crinkly, white-backed leaves. The bush is armed with stout thorns, but the hairy, almost black raspberries are delicious and worth a few scratches. This fruit was a favourite of aboriginal peoples, who dried them and made them into cakes. The young shoots were peeled and eaten too, and an infusion from the boiled roots was taken for influenza.

A common berry that is not so good to eat is the fruit of the red elderberry. These coarse, rangy shrubs are ubiquitous on our coast, often growing to a great height. The large leaves have several pointed leaflets and in May heads of yellowish-white flowers appear, accompanied by a pungent smell and soon to be followed by clusters of smooth red berries. These are not considered edible and may be harmful. The saying "He who cultivates the elderberry will live until an old age and die in his own bed" evidently refers only to the blue elderberry. Black twinberry too, which you might come across in the ravine, is best left untasted. This straggly member of the honeysuckle family is usually found in damp places. It is recognizable by its long, pale-green leaves and twinned, tubular yellow flowers. The fruit, appearing in July or August, is distinctive—two shiny black berries cupped in two pairs of sticky, reddish bracts. Some aboriginal peoples ascribed various curses to the eating of twinberries, such as loss of speech, but these baneful influences did not discourage the Haida from rubbing the berries into their hair to prevent it from turning grey.

If you peer through the trees at just the right place in your gentle descent along the eastside trail, you can spot the beginning of the famous stairway across the ravine. Presently, the sound of traffic on Marine Drive reaches you, and you find yourself out in the open, wandering over the site of long-gone homes. Old fruit trees stand sadly in rough grass that is dotted with grape hyacinths gone wild; ivy and periwinkle run amok over the remains of a rockery. Between the rampant forsythia bushes you step out onto Marine Drive, a few hundred metres east of the trailhead. Nature walkers hope this right-of-way will be preserved when the long arm of development reaches this corner of Byrne Creek ravine.

HOW TO GET THERE: The signposted trailhead is on the north side of southeast Marine Drive in Burnaby, a few metres east of Gilley Avenue. There is limited parking space. Journey time: 20 minutes. By bus: Take the No. 100 from Marpole Loop or No. 114 from Metrotown Station to Gilley and Marine.

8
Shoreline Trail

HIGHLIGHTS
Tidal marsh, forest; historic sites, fish hatchery; ducks, shorebirds, raptors

SEASON
All year

ROUND TRIP
Noons Creek 3 km (2 miles); Old Orchard Park 6 km (3¾ miles)

TERRAIN
Flat. Forest trails and boardwalks. Rocky Point Park paths are suitable for wheelchairs.

FAMILY WALK
Rocky Point Park offers a playground, pool and picnic tables. Learn about Port Moody's railway history at the Station Museum on Murray Street.

CONGRATULATIONS TO the City of Port Moody for preserving the waterfront at the head of Burrard Inlet for recreation, thus blessing wildlife and other lovers of the outdoors. The 3-km (2-mile) Shoreline Trail from Rocky Point Park to Old Orchard Park on the north side of Port Moody Arm offers interest throughout the year, and the addition of a separate cycle track enhances the pleasure for all concerned.

Shoreline Trail can be picked up on the east side of the park, past the playground. After crossing the gruesomely named Slaughterhouse Creek, the "walkers only" trail branches left into the forest. Many tall evergreens remain, towering from a forest floor luxuriant with salal and sword fern, and in spring, bracken, wood fern and false lily-of-the-valley. You will pass the shell and ribs of an old fish packer abandoned to the mud long since, a sapling now growing out of its decaying hull. A little farther along, a viewing platform gives you the chance to observe the bird life of the estuary. Mallards, widgeon, pintails, mergansers and the small green-winged teal are among the many ducks found here in fall and winter, along with various shorebirds and our ubiquitous Canada geese. And to remind you that this is the seaside, several species of gulls frequent the rich feeding ground of the estuary.

Presently you come to the mouth of Suter Brook, where you venture over the marsh on a long, zigzag boardwalk. Tall sedges flank the way in summer, but in winter the boards are high above the flattened vegetation.

Several small streams flow into the estuary. Middens discovered at the mouth of Noons Creek indicate that aboriginal people used to camp there during salmon spawning. Although the original salmon runs were lost as development intruded, local residents, now under the name of Port Moody Ecological Society, built and operate a small hatchery beside the creek, raising chum and coho salmon. A short side trail heading upstream from the Noons Creek bridge leads to the hatchery, where volunteers may be on hand to show visitors the rearing ponds or, depending on the season, the trays of incubating eggs, each salmon-pink blob endowed with a single eye. Herons, ospreys, bald eagles and kingfishers can be seen hunting around the estuary. Harbour seals are frequent visitors too, particularly during spawning time.

The mudflats that form where a river or stream deposits its sediment into a sheltered bay present what can seem at first a desolate scene, especially at low tide. Rivulets and channels lie between tussocks of salt-grass; debris and driftwood poke out of the rippled brown mud that extends to the shallow water farther out. The river and the tide take turns depositing or sweeping away their respective offerings of silt, debris and organisms to produce an everchanging ecosystem, sometimes wet and sometimes dry, a constant mingling of salt water and fresh.

But this confusing habitat teems with life. Worms, snails, clams and crustaceans are some of the highly specialized creatures equipped for a drifting or burrowing life in the mud. Able to breathe without gills in their opaque surroundings and feed on plankton (microscopic organisms brought in by the sea), these tiny animals survive in their fluid environment until they, in their turn, become part of the food web. Sandpipers and dunlin dash energetically around the mudflats stabbing for burrowers just below the surface; greater yellowlegs and long-billed dowitchers wade thigh-high to probe for deeper inhabitants. From overhead, the great blue heron flaps majestically down to pursue its own style of hunting—a patient, stealthy stalking of fish or crustacean to add to its varied diet of frogs, mice and insects.

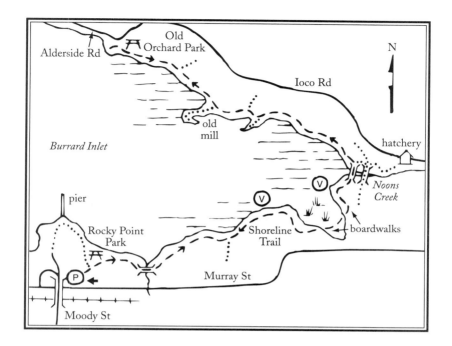

Beyond Noons Creek the trail becomes less formal as it follows the northern shore of Port Moody Arm. Songbirds are more evident as you walk through the narrow strip of woodland along the foreshore, and by early summer you might spot Wilson's and orange-crowned warblers along with the resident wrens, chickadees and bushtits. Several access paths join the trail from the roads above. It is pleasant walking nonetheless, and an interesting side trip can be made to the site of an old cedar shingle mill. Watch the tide here if you decide to pick your way over the spongy ground to explore the derelict buildings.

After passing through a poplar grove, the trail comes to its final destination in Old Orchard Park, where picnic tables and a sandy beach invite you to stay a while before retracing your steps to Rocky Point.

HOW TO GET THERE: From St. John's Street (Highway 7A) in Port Moody, turn north on Moody Street. After crossing the railway on the overpass, turn left at the stop sign onto Murray Street and proceed to the Rocky Point parking lot on the left. Journey time: 40 minutes. By bus: Take the No. 160 from the Kootenay Loop or the No. 147 or 148 from New Westminster Station.

9
Buntzen Lake

HIGHLIGHTS
Lake, forest, mountains; fungi; sapsuckers

SEASON
All year

ROUND TRIP
1.5 km (1 mile). Optional side trip to the floating bridge is an additional 1.2 km (¾ mile).

TERRAIN
Gentle ups and downs. Well-groomed forest trail, mostly gravel.

FAMILY WALK
There is a well-furnished picnic area, spacious beach and playing field; also a launching ramp for car-top boats and canoes. Power boats are prohibited.

LAKE BEAUTIFUL, as this body of water was originally called, was dammed in 1903 as part of Vancouver's first hydroelectric power project. Later, a tunnel was made through Eagle Mountain (the outflow can be seen at North Beach) bringing water from Coquitlam Lake, and a power plant was built on Indian Arm. By this time the reservoir had been renamed after the general manager of B.C. Electric, Johannes Buntzen, a change that could not detract from the beauty of the 5-km (3-mile)–long lake lying between the forested slopes of Buntzen Ridge and Eagle Mountain, above Indian Arm.

B.C. Hydro maintains an excellent hiking trail that encircles the lake, as well as the Energy Nature Trail described here and other paths that link up with trails on Buntzen Ridge. Hikers can also use the network of equestrian trails surrounding the lake or undertake the strenuous Eagle Ridge trails made by Vancouver's pioneer of hiking and climbing routes, Halvor Lunden.

Buntzen Lake

I have chosen the Energy Trail more for its interesting natural features than for its views—the region's stunning scenery can be appreciated from South Beach or from a viewpoint on the east side of the lake, easily reached by a fifteen-minute walk. The nature trail is particularly rewarding in fall, especially after heavy rain, when many fascinating mushrooms appear on the dead wood and push their way up through the duff.

To find the trailhead, follow the paved road that heads left from the third parking lot, along the southwest side of the picnic area. Ignore the

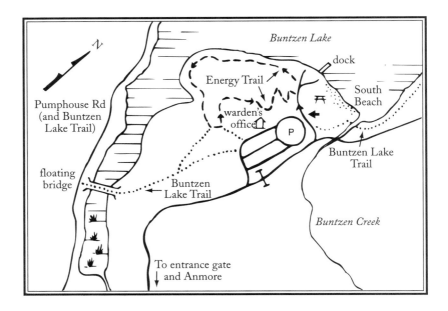

In the map:

Buntzen Lake

dock

Energy Trail

South Beach

Pumphouse Rd
(and Buntzen
Lake Trail)

warden's
office

P

Buntzen Lake
Trail

floating
bridge

Buntzen
Lake Trail

Buntzen Creek

To entrance gate
and Anmore

first Energy Trail sign and continue towards the boat launching ramp, where you'll see an information board and map. Panels expounding on the energy theme are situated along the trail, though by the end of the summer some might have been removed for cleaning or repair. The gravel path winds through the forest along the lake's eastern shore, giving glimpses of the water through the fringe of trees.

If the season and conditions are appropriate, start looking for mushrooms right away. They are not easy to identify, even with a pocket guide, but this does not lessen their beauty or the fascination they hold for us. Some I have been fairly sure of along here are *Lactarius deliciosus* (don't be tempted to nibble any of them) with a large orange-brown cap and paler gills crowding down the stalk; colonies of snow-white angel wings attached to rotting conifer logs; and warm-hued orange lactarius scattered around the base of hemlock trees. The visible mushroom, consisting of cap and stalk, is not the whole picture, but simply the fruiting body of the main plant, which is a mass of threadlike growths called the mycelium that remains embedded in the soil or material it is feeding on below the ground. When conditions are right, the above-ground form is produced, ready to release its spores from gills or pores beneath the cap. The tiny spores can be carried far by the wind, but some fungi are selective and grow only on a particular plant or site, so not all wandering spores find a home.

Lacking green chlorophyll, fungi cannot utilize sunlight to make food as other plants do, but must take their nourishment from food already stored in organic material—as we animals do. Thus, fungi act as waste-disposers, breaking down the substance of logs and leaves and converting it back into soil and air, setting an example of efficient recycling. Don't expect to find many perfect fungus specimens on your walk through the woods—slugs, insects, squirrels, rabbits and deer are all partial to a mushroom snack.

At the edge of a chaotic blowdown area, where salal, huckleberry and tree seedlings are taking advantage of the additional light, you might notice a large fallen cedar close to the shore. Its upturned root disk has exposed a bed of rock, showing how shallow-rooted the great trees of the coastal rainforest are. Farther along, a standing dead hemlock with a grotesquely bulging trunk and a severe case of parasitic witches' broom is being further devastated by woodpeckers. The pileated woodpecker is a forest's primary excavator, speeding up the decay of rotting stumps and snags with its large, rectangular workings. The smaller downy woodpecker does its share, chiselling its way into insect tunnels, while the sapsucker sticks to its own unique method of getting sustenance from a living tree.

Our west coast sapsucker is easily recognized by its bright red head, neck and breast. The belly is yellowish, the wings and back mostly black. A white patch on the side of the folded wing is the hallmark of all sapsuckers. I once watched a red-breasted sapsucker on the Energy Trail, working its way up, down and sideways on the trunk of a hemlock, barely two metres from where I stood. Its strategy is to drill rows of shallow holes in the bark, which then fill with sap plus a cargo of insects, which the bird picks up with a brush-tipped tongue. Other birds, and even squirrels, may help themselves at sapsucker wells.

As the trail bends left through an area of feathery young hemlocks, you will come to a side trail descending to the right, opposite a blue Energy Trail sign. You can, if you wish, take this right-hand path to join the Buntzen Lake Trail on its way to cross the floating bridge over the narrow panhandle of the lake. Skunk cabbage, hardhack, buckbean and water lilies can be seen from the boardwalk; drowned trees and stumps signify the reservoir's changing water levels.

Resuming your circuit along the Energy Trail, you will begin to see many large cedar stumps as the path swings northward in the lee of some rocky outcroppings and wooded hummocks. Then, after a beautiful glade of deer fern, tall hemlocks close in to shut out the light, a scattering of nutrient-starved plants struggling to survive beneath them. The giant stumps loom impassively on either side, prompting one to wonder what those first woodsmen felt when they entered the glades with their axes and crosscut saws.

When a forest is disturbed, by fire or storm or logging, nature sets about the process of regeneration right away. Into the open spaces seeds of grasses and flowers are blown; deer and grouse will venture there to feed. In a year or two there are shrubs big enough to provide food and cover for birds and small mammals. In ten more years young trees have formed a leafy ceiling above the shrubs; squirrels and a few tree-nesting birds arrive. Over the next, much longer period, as the trees grow taller and the canopy thickens, the ground is cast into deep shade and ground vegetation declines. Many inhabitants move away, leaving the forest to birds who feed on conifer seeds and insects.

Gradually, competition breaks the deadlock. Weaker trees fall, letting light through the canopy so that plants can grow again. Fungi do their work on the increasing debris, enriching the soil for deciduous shrubs. Wildlife returns. In time, perhaps a century or two after the fire or disturbance, some of the largest trees will have fallen, the logs providing a habitat for countless insects, birds and mammals and a nursery for tree seedlings. There will be standing dead trees also, where cavity-nesting creatures live, and high tree-top sites for ravens and eagles. A mature forest has evolved, with stands of giant conifers, open spaces, and layers of understorey rich in wildlife.

Energy Trail winds downhill past a viewing platform to emerge on the service road opposite the round picnic shelter. Don't sheath your observation skills too soon, though—clusters of inky cap mushrooms may be growing around the base of the triple-trunked broadleaf maple on the left of the road.

HOW TO GET THERE: From Highway 7A (Barnet Highway) in Port Moody, take the Ioco exit. Follow Ioco Road to the left and continue for about 4 km (2½ miles) to a right turn on 1st Avenue, opposite Ioco United Church. Turn right again on Sunnyside Road to Anmore and proceed through the Buntzen Lake Reservoir entrance gate to the third (last) parking lot at South Beach. Journey time: 1 hour.

10
Mundy Park

COQUITLAM

HIGHLIGHTS
Forest and lake; nurse stumps; ferns, wildflowers, bog plants; woodland birds

SEASON
All year

ROUND TRIP
2.4 km (1½ miles)

TERRAIN
Flat. Sawdust and gravel trails.

FAMILY WALK
Look for bat shelters (they look like bird nesting boxes) fastened high on tree trunks; fish for bullheads at Mundy Lake.

MUNDY PARK IS UNDOUBTEDLY Coquitlam's great oasis. The 190 ha (435 acres) of coniferous and deciduous forest atop Austin Heights have been left virtually undisturbed since they were logged at the turn of the century. Beyond the fringe of recreation facilities along the park's western boundary, hundred-year-old Douglas firs, cedars and hemlocks tower over an understorey of alder, birch and vine maple. The two small lakes in the park are fringed with swamp laurel and Labrador tea, and support rare swamp and king gentians.

Of the 12 km (7 miles) of level, well-kept trails that lace the park, I have described only a few—a short sampling of forest and lake, leaving plenty to explore on subsequent visits. The trails are named (they were originally coded by colour; you might notice the blue, red and orange markers on the trees), and maps are placed at strategic points to keep the walker on track. As well as the Hillcrest Street entrance, there is access to the park from Austin Avenue, Como Lake Avenue to the north and Mariner Way on the east side. Don't hesitate to choose

Mundy Park for a winter walk; the sawdust trails are kind even when frozen, and when snow fills every hollow and lines every twig there is a cathedral hush to the forest aisles.

Head east from the parking lot, towards the big trees. Opposite the end of a playing field, Perimeter Trail heads right (south) to begin its circular route around the park. An extraordinary hemlock stands at this junction, a tree whose life began on an old stump now almost gone, so that roots which once held tight to the nurse now stand unsupported, the whole structure worn smooth by the hands and feet of appreciative children. Peace descends as you follow the path down between borders of salmonberry bushes to cross the outlet stream from Mundy Lake. In spring, sword ferns send up their strong new shoots among a froth of delicate wood fern; trilliums and yellow violets find quieter spaces on the forest floor to display their beauty.

Walking eastward beneath the tall trees, you will surely become aware of birdsong all around you—the cheerful caroling of a robin, the trilling of a summer warbler or, best of all, the flutelike phrases of a hermit thrush trying out its music in various pitches. Two forest residents not often heard or spotted are the brown creeper and the red-breasted nuthatch. The latter is a small, short-tailed bird, blue-grey above, buff- or reddish-breasted, with a black cap and white stripe above the eye. It works over the trunk and twigs of a tree, headfirst up and down, in its search for seeds and insects. The brown creeper tackles the job differently. Clinging with long claws, its sharply pointed tail flattened against the tree trunk, this bird spirals up the tree in a series of jerky movements as it forages for insects. When that patch is picked over, it flies to the base of another tree to begin again the upward spiral. It is not easy to witness this intriguing performance as the streaked and speckled brown bird so resembles the bark that is the mainstay of its life. As well as providing the insects on which the bird feeds, a loose piece of bark serves the brown creeper well at nesting time. Into the crescent-shaped space behind, a nest of twigs, leaves and bark shreddings is fitted, lined inside with moss and more bark, finely shredded.

Shortly after passing a long nurse log beside the path, you will come to a junction. Leaving the lengthy Perimeter Trail for another time, turn left onto Waterline Trail. As you penetrate deeper into the heart of the forest, the story of its regeneration is very evident. Here and there among the second-growth timber, the stumps of thousand-year-old spruce, cedars and Douglas firs host new generations of shrubs and trees. Imagine that old stump or log in the first year of its demise:

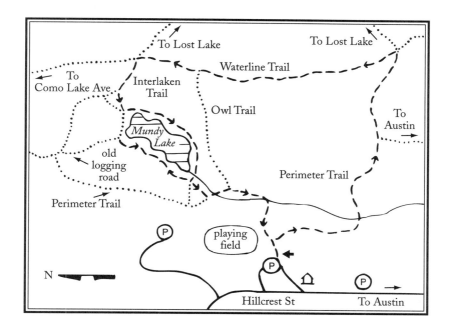

woodlice, slugs and centipedes will soon find shelter there. By the following year, beetles and spiders take up residence, and fungi and mosses begin to establish themselves on the decaying wood. Wood-boring insects, which help things along by riddling the log with holes, in their turn become the food for visiting woodpeckers. Soon flowers begin to grow on the log, then shrubs, privileged plants that are spared the competition of existence on the forest floor by the ready source of food and water supplied by the nurse. And gradually, finally, the fallen giant that gave birth to this self-supporting society returns to the soil, its story told.

Keep straight ahead on Waterline where Owl Trail joins on the left, and continue until you meet a gravel road, where a sign directs you left to Mundy Lake, the highlight of your tour. Immediately after passing a grassy picnic area on the right, you will arrive at the north end of the lake, with a view opening out between the huckleberry bushes. The left-hand path follows the eastern lakeshore closely, bringing you to a landing at the south end, near which an upturned tree presents a unique view of its root system, adorned at the top with a cape of moss and flowers upheaved by the fall.

From here, the path heading left, away from the water, will soon take you back to your starting point, but first take a stroll along the west side

of the lake. This shoreline is fringed with shore pines, huckleberry, Labrador tea and swamp laurel. The ground at the water's edge is spongy and peaty. In fact, Mundy Lake is slowly being filled in by sphagnum moss and is on its way to becoming a peat bog. Some benches are provided for contemplation, as well as a fishing dock for anglers who hope for a small trout among the bullheads and catfish. Mallards and buffleheads frequent the lake; on one occasion a worldly-wise mallard drake slid out from the reeds as I approached and paddled alongside me for an entire circuit of the lake. Frogs, toads, salamanders and garter snakes might also be found in the vicinity—a fact well-known by visiting herons.

When you are ready to head for home, return to the south end of Mundy Lake and follow the path east from the landing. Turn left when you meet Perimeter Trail and thereafter follow the sign to Hillcrest Street. When you are ready to explore other trails in the park, you might like to contact the Friends of Mundy Park Society, in Coquitlam, for one of their excellent nature trail guidebooks.

HOW TO GET THERE: From Highway 7 (Lougheed Highway), turn left on Austin Road in Coquitlam. After passing the Lougheed Mall and crossing North Road, continue on Austin (now Austin Avenue) for a further 4 km (2½ miles) to Hillcrest Street. Turn left here. Ignore the first parking area on the right but turn in at the Mundy Park sign a few metres farther along. Follow the access road to the main parking area. Journey time: 30 minutes.

By bus: Take the No. 152 from the Kootenay Loop to Austin and Hillcrest. Walk north on Hillcrest Street to the park.

FACING PAGE: *Nurse log*

11
Minnekhada

MINNEKHADA REGIONAL PARK

COQUITLAM

HIGHLIGHTS
Freshwater marsh, forest, rocky knolls; Minnekhada Lodge; waterfowl, raptors, songbirds; bullfrogs

SEASON
All year

ROUND TRIP
2 km (1 ¼ miles) or 3.4 km (2 miles)

TERRAIN
Short walk is mainly flat with minor ups and downs, on forest trail and dyke. Complete circuit includes some climbing and rougher sections.

FAMILY WALK
For the adventurous, Minnekhada's rocky knolls will be irresistible destinations. Others will be content to end their walk with a picnic beside the marsh, below the lodge.

NOW ONE OF THE MOST DELIGHTFUL of our regional parks, the 219 ha (548 acres) of marsh, forest and farmland at the foot of Burke Mountain were once a private hunting preserve, created and used by two former lieutenant governors of British Columbia. The rustic hunting lodge, built in 1934, is open on certain Sunday afternoons from February to December and can be booked for private occasions. The buildings of Minnekhada Farm, added to the park in 1995, are being restored and will eventually be made accessible to the public.

From the park's eastern boundary, trails connect with the Addington Marsh Wildlife Management Area bordering the Pitt River, and with De Bouville Slough to the south. Ten km (6 miles) of walking trails encircle and dissect the park, exploring coniferous forest and alder woods, the 185-m (550-foot) High Knoll and the central marshes. For those who prefer gentle terrain, I suggest the short walk from the lodge

Broadleaf maple flowers

to the east end of the dyke and back; others can continue to the Low Knoll, then pick up the perimeter trail to complete a circular walk. The most convenient starting point for both walks is the lodge parking lot, but should this be reserved for a private function, you will see from the map that short trails from the Quarry Road entrance connect with the suggested route.

I have described the walk in mid-May to mid-June, when baby swallows are peeping from the nestboxes and the marsh resounds with froggy love songs, but do visit Minnekhada at other times of year. Winter sees the north marsh alive with ring-necked ducks, buffleheads, shovelers, widgeon, mergansers and green-winged teal. Red-tailed hawks and Northern harriers are joined in winter by sharp-shinned and Cooper's hawks, merlins and sometimes American kestrels. By February great horned owls will have begun to build their nests in the forest east of the lodge.

From the lodge parking lot, walk back down the drive for a few metres until you see a grassy area with picnic tables, below a bend in the road. Head left (west) along the trail from here, at first through forest, then into the open to cross a bridge over the tail end of the lower, or south, marsh. The cedar-chip trail now turns north along a dyke, and this is where you might become aware of the "jug-a-rum" chorus of the bullfrogs. During their long breeding period the males float on the surface, flaunting their yellow throats to rivals, and interrupting their territorial announcements only to grab any tempting female who hops into their parlour. The green or olive-brown aquatic bullfrog is easily identified by its great size, slightly humped back and prominent eardrums. The greenish tadpoles, too, are larger than those of other species, and can be 15 cm (6 inches) at maturity. Adult frogs are voracious feeders, gulping down insects, mice, fish, even young birds and smaller frogs. Their own fate can be just as harsh—they can be snatched from a lily pad by a marsh hawk and borne aloft, legs dangling, to be presented to a nest of raptor chicks as dinner. Many others slide to oblivion down herons' gullets.

The trail reenters the woods at the end of the dyke, climbing a few metres above marsh level. Keeping right where trails from Quarry Road join, you will soon arrive at a viewpoint from which you can gaze across the divided marsh to the rocky outcropping of Low Knoll and the sterner High Knoll beyond. From this vantage point, you will see that the north marsh is largely open water while the area south of the central dyke supports more sedges and spirea, the whole providing habitats for a variety of birds and animals. For a close-up of this rich environment, take the path descending to marsh level and stroll eastward along the main dyke.

Red-winged blackbirds, flycatchers and warblers forage among the shrubs. A disapproving "tsick, tsick" means you have disturbed a common yellowthroat in its search for aphids and caterpillars. This little warbler fusses about like a wren among the sedges and spirea, the male easy to recognize by its distinctive, black highwayman's mask.

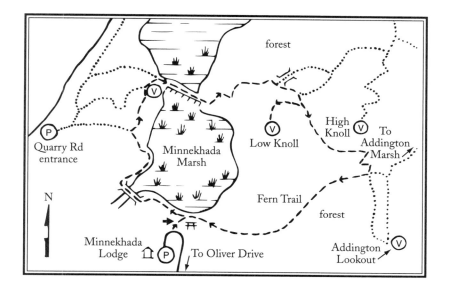

Dragonflies and mayflies dart and hover over the grasses; two mallards take off with a whirr of wings; a muskrat leaves the bank with a plop and trails a V-shaped wake through the water.

Among the diving birds that frequent the marsh in spring and summer is the shy but accomplished pied-billed grebe. This plain little grebe with a stout, henlike bill can submerge without a ripple, usually while you are getting your binoculars focussed. Using wings and feet to swim underwater, it pursues its diet of fish and crustaceans. Waiting for the diver to surface can be frustrating, as this canny bird is capable of sneaking along with only its eyes and nostrils above the water. Like the coot, the pied-billed grebe builds a floating nest of sticks and vegetation, a home that can adapt to the fluctuating water level of a marsh. The clever parent can carry the chicks upon its back and even dive with them. It seems that the only thing a grebe does not do well is move on land. The legs of a diving bird are set well back on its body for underwater thrust, but this design is not helpful for walking, and the bird is apt to pitch forward on its chest, resorting when panicked to ungainly wing-flapping to get along—a pitiful manoeuvre compared with its speed and grace in the water.

The dyke ends abruptly on the east side of the marsh, and many will choose to turn around here and retrace their steps to the lodge. Those who can take some rocks and roots in their stride can stay with the trail as it ascends through Douglas firs and cedars towards the looming bulk of High Knoll. Keep an eye out for the occasional red marker as you pick your way over the rocky hummocks. After a sharp change of direction to the left and a descent through young hemlocks, you will pass cliffs on the right, before arriving at a trail junction. Ignoring the left-hand trail with its bridge, keep right to reach a second junction where a big old cedar snag stands guard. Go right again (you are now on the perimeter trail) and in a few minutes you will come to the side trail to Low Knoll. This is a short and easy diversion, well worth the little effort it takes, but one word of caution: if there are children in your party, don't let them run ahead—the drop-off at the viewpoint is considerable and abruptly come upon.

From the modest west-facing knoll, with its firs and carpet of kinnikinnick, you can survey the south marsh, the long ridge of Burke Mountain and, on a clear day, the Alex Fraser bridge and the towers of Guildford on the skyline. Standing alone at this viewpoint one day (having already climbed High Knoll, my companions elected to wait for me below), I was joined by an exquisite little bird. Field glasses were unnecessary, for it alighted on a branch only two metres away, from where it regarded me steadily for several minutes, not alarmed even when I pulled a notebook from my pocket and proceeded to make an annotated sketch: brilliant red head, yellow body, black wings and tail. "A tropical bird," I wrote, and indeed it was, for I identified it later as a western tanager, arrived on its Canadian breeding grounds from its wintering ground in Mexico or South America.

Returning to the main trail, proceed to the right. After passing some giant nurse logs and picking your way down a stony incline, the terrain becomes gentler as the rugged cliffs of High Knoll are left behind. After connecting trails to Addington Marsh and Addington Point Lookout are passed on the left, your homeward route swings westward, through forest that is home to woodpeckers, owls and Steller's jays, as well as larger and shyer inhabitants such as coyotes, bears and black-tailed deer. You walk beneath mossy branches, over a stretch of old skid road, and eventually step out of the trees into the grassy picnic area below the lodge drive, your circuit completed.

HOW TO GET THERE: From Highway 7 (Lougheed Highway), turn north on Coast Meridian Road. In 2.5 km (1½ miles) go right on Apel Drive and follow park signs to Minnekhada Lodge. Journey time: 1 hour.

12
Colony Farm

HIGHLIGHTS
River and old farmlands; waterfowl, herons, hawks, songbirds; beaver
workings; coyotes

SEASON
All year

ROUND TRIP
West side: up to 6.5 km (4 miles)
East side: 4 km (2 ½ miles)

TERRAIN
Flat. Dyke-top and footpath.

FAMILY WALK
Combine this outing with a self-guided tour of nearby Riverview
arboretum, Western Canada's first botanical garden. Information stand
is just off Lougheed Highway east of Colony Farm Road.

ONCE A PRODUCTIVE FARM operated by the patients of Riverview
Hospital, Colony Farm lands extend along both sides of the Coquitlam
River between its confluence with the Fraser and Indian Reserve No. 2 at
Pitt River Road. Since the closure of the farm by the government in 1985,
the lands have been threatened repeatedly by development, saved only by
community opposition and the efforts of organizations such as the Burke
Mountain Naturalists Society. Thanks to their perseverance, Colony
Farm has now become a Greater Vancouver Regional District park,
thereby destined to remain a green oasis in the surrounding desert of
subdivisions. The area is a prime bird-watching site year round, and the
walker on the dykes will soon forget the sound of traffic from nearby
roads and railway. Binoculars are an asset on this walk. Since the lands are
divided by the Coquitlam River and the connecting bridge has fallen
prey to time and vandals, I have described the two sides as separate walks.

For the westside walk, head left from the Colony Road parking lot, go across the bridge over the ditch and follow the dyke path through the red gate. Eventually the dyke converges with the river, beside which you wend your way upstream. Great blue herons are so plentiful on these flatlands that one wonders how many mice, frogs and fishes ever attain old age. I have counted as many as eighteen herons at one time, winging their way from the old bridge site towards the heronry in the cotton-woods at the rivermouth. The less common green-backed heron has also been sighted in Colony Farm ditches, most often in summer or fall. The dark colour and secretive manner of this smaller heron make it difficult to spot, but a glimpse of its bright yellow legs might betray its presence.

Each season brings its own colour to the dykes and fields. The purple lupins of spring are followed by fields of yellow buttercups. Oxeye daisies, fireweed and orange and yellow hawkweed take over, and by August brilliant blue chicory flowers catch the eye, waving on their tall stems above tansy and Douglas asters. As the pink and purple thistle flowers fade, flocks of bright yellow and black goldfinches swoop down to feast upon the seeds.

Don't be discouraged to find yourself converging with Highway 7 and the railway, but continue northward on the footpath created by the enterprising Burke Mountain Naturalists. The scene changes. From an outer fringe of bushes and brambles, you enter a narrow belt of wood-land, where birch, maple and alder are dominated by tall black cotton-woods. Beavers are making their mark here and have already toppled several large trees. There are many openings from which you can observe the river as you wind your way upstream to the trail's end at a rock-lined channel, made to provide a resting place for young salmon. On the other side of the channel is Pitt River Road and the site of a Bailey bridge spanning the Coquitlam River. At the time of writing, the Red Bridge, as it was known locally, is being replaced by a grander structure better able to withstand the frequent flooding of the river. This is your turnaround point for the westside walk.

The eastside walk: Having found your way to the trailhead on Mary Hill Road, set off down the slope to join the dyke heading west towards the river. On a winter walk you might see pintails, bufflehead, mergansers and green-winged teal among the resident mallards and Canada geese in this marshy area. Winter is also a good time to watch for raptors: bald eagles and red-tailed hawks soar and circle over the farmlands in their search for small mammals; the little American kestrel

Thistle

keeps an eye on rodent activity from a pole or fence post. The Northern harrier glides low over the marsh on slender, pointed wings, head bowed as it inspects the ground for frogs and field mice. A white rump patch distinguishes this marsh hawk from others.

The courtship dance of the Northern harrier is thrilling to behold, the male hawk climbing to sixty feet or more, then plunging earthward in a series of cartwheels. Sometimes, prey is passed in midair from the

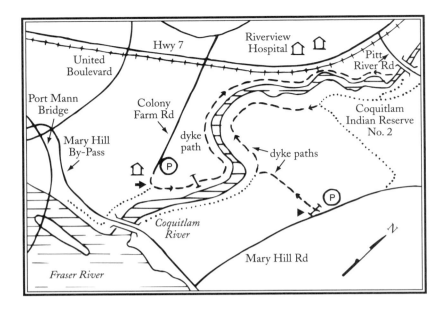

male to its mate, or dropped for her to catch on the wing. Courtship feeding is common in birds of prey. A female gull, for instance, may be presented with a regurgitated morsel; more romantically, the snowy owl positions himself upon a mound or log, where he displays the gift against his outspread wings.

Soon you arrive at the main dyke along the Coquitlam River. Turn right and walk upstream beside the thickets of salmonberry, elderberry, wild roses and willows bordering the river. The colours, even in February or March, are exquisite along this stretch: parchment-coloured winter grasses, sepia willow twigs blushed with yellow and red, the dry, brown heads of hardhack, and here and there an unfurling green leaf and drooping white blossom of Indian plum.

In summer, band-tailed pigeons and cedar waxwings feed on the red elderberries; warblers and flycatchers join song sparrows, chickadees and bushtits among the waterside shrubs. The rufous hummingbird is a common spring and summer visitor; if you are lucky, a flash of blue might signify a glimpse of the rare lazuli bunting or mountain bluebird, both of which have been sighted at Colony Farm in recent years.

As the dyke turns slightly eastward, a belt of tangled, swampy woodland claims the widening space between path and river. Tall cottonwoods and conifers provide a habitat for finches and woodpeckers. On the landward side, a ditch with cattails is a favourite hunting place for herons. When you meet a wide gravel road, you have reached the edge of Indian Reserve No. 2. By following the dyke heading east, you will find yourself back on Mary Hill Road with a fifteen-minute walk along the blacktop to your car. A better way is to retrace your steps along the river, where there is still much to be seen, but before you turn around, scan the open fields for hunting hawks or coyotes.

While resting here one day in early March, I spotted a lone coyote. The loping gait, the hanging bushy tail and pointed face were unmistakeable as it ran unhurriedly, with a characteristic mixture of boldness and caution, across the open field. It stopped frequently and abruptly, always in a patch of shadowed or darker ground, so that it seemed to vanish on the instant, invisible until it travelled on.

This intelligence, combined with keen hearing, sight and smell, is the secret of the coyote's survival. It knows how to keep out of traps and gunshot range. It will eat insects, carrion and vegetation if small mammals and birds are scarce, but it is wise about poison. It often mates for life and diligently raises a large family—a family which may later hunt together with great resourcefulness. The coyote's song at night has been described as "a prolonged howl which the animal let out and then ran after and bit into small pieces." Coyotes deserve a place on Colony Farm's wild acres.

HOW TO GET THERE: To westside dykes: From Highway 7 (Lougheed Highway) in Coquitlam, turn south on Colony Farm Road, about 800 m (½ mile) east of United Boulevard. Drive to the parking area near the forensic buildings at the end of the road. Journey time: 30 minutes.

To eastside dykes: From Highway 7 in Coquitlam, turn south on United Boulevard and follow signs to Pitt Meadows, Maple Ridge and Mission (the Mary Hill bypass). Or, leave Highway 1 at exit 44 and follow similar signs to the bypass. Turn left (north) on Mary Hill Road and drive for about 1.2 km (¾ mile) to a small parking area beside the Colony Farm trail sign and gate. Journey time: 30 minutes.

13
Pitt Marshes

PITT WILDLIFE MANAGEMENT AREA
MAPLE RIDGE

HIGHLIGHTS
Pitt Lake, freshwater marsh; mountain views; waterfowl, ospreys, eagles, swans, songbirds; beavers

SEASON
All year. Winter best for waterfowl.

ROUND TRIP
5.6 km (3 ½ miles)

TERRAIN
Flat. Dyke-top paths, one narrow and wooded.

FAMILY WALK
There are boating and picnicking facilities at Grant Narrows, and a food concession on summer weekends.

PITT POLDER, through which you drive on your way to Pitt Lake, has been dyked and drained at different periods since the 1870s, the main reclamation being made by Dutch settlers in the early 1950s. To the north, between farmland and lake, 1500 ha (3750 acres) of water and marsh are preserved as a sanctuary for wildlife. Although the Pitt River and the lake are tidal, a system of dykes and pumphouses controlling the water levels counteracts brackishness and has enabled freshwater marsh and spirea bog to develop. To encourage waterfowl, grass and plants have been allowed to grow and nesting areas have been built, protected from people and predators by canals; water management schemes of beavers and muskrats are kept in check. Minks, foxes, coyotes, bears and deer visit or inhabit the area.

There is no dull season on the marsh. In the winter months you'll see, among others, widgeon, pintail, gadwall, goldeneyes, grebes and mergansers, and tundra and trumpeter swans. Woodland birds frequent the shrubby areas year-round, while swallows, warblers and flycatchers

Beaver lodge

arrive with the warmer weather. Raptors can be seen at most times. The marsh itself changes with the seasons too, the winter monochrome giving way to a range of browns, greens and blues, subtly enhanced by reflections, and frost-whitened dyke tops become narrow paths between waist-high grass entwined with wildflowers. The backdrop of mountains is breathtaking whether capped with snow, shrouded in mist, or starkly blue against a threatening sky.

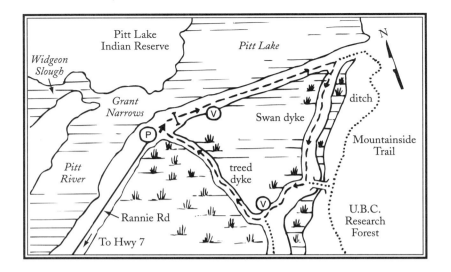

And that brings us to the weather. Cold winds can sweep down Pitt Lake, making you want to pull your head in like a snail, so dress warmly for a winter outing. In summer, you may long for shade on the open dykes, or for the breeze that cannot reach you for the surrounding tall grass; take a hat and some water. And do take binoculars at any time.

Grant Narrows, now a regional park, can be a lively scene on summer weekends, with boaters putting their crafts in the water and adventurers setting out in canoes to explore the channels of Widgeon Creek across the river. Head out through the gate onto the main Pitt Lake dyke to begin a circular, or perhaps triangular, tour of the northern part of the marsh. At first, the lake and its surrounding mountains steal all one's attention. Ahead of you to the east are the wooded slopes of the University of British Columbia Research Forest; to the northeast the peaks of Golden Ears and Garibaldi park form a rampart around the northern end of the lake, and the long ridge of Burke Mountain encloses the valley to the west. Scoured by the ice age, the lake stretches for 26 km (16 miles), draining from the region between Squamish and Whistler and emptying into the Pitt River at Grant Narrows.

When you can spare an eye for things closer at hand, watch for resident ospreys fishing over the marsh. Their untidy nests of sticks and debris are on the tops of several pilings at the edge of the lake. When there are young to feed, the male hunts throughout the day. The large, torpedo-shaped hawk hovers over the marsh, then plummets to the water, angled back wings snapping open at the last moment, legs driving down to snatch the unwary fish with four sharp talons. Long, slender wings lift the bird from the water, and before the spray has settled it is heading for home with its prize grasped firmly by head and tail. Tiny spines on the osprey's feet enable it to hold onto its slippery prey. With binoculars, from the observation tower on the dyke, you might be able to watch the family at dinner.

Near the end of Pitt Lake dyke, turn right onto Swan dyke and proceed southward along the edge of the marsh. This is the domain of the red-winged blackbird and his shyer, brown-streaked mate. Ducks and geese are busy everywhere—I have counted six families of geese with downy goslings in the ditch on the left of the dyke—and swans can usually be seen farther out on the water. In early summer, lupins, columbine and dame's violet mingle with the tall grass beside the path. When you reach the belt of cottonwood trees, make for the observation tower ahead.

Looking southward from the platform, you will see that the marsh supports areas of vegetation between minor dykes and channels, and that beyond the next observation tower the surface is dotted with nesting islands. As well as the dyke running along the eastern boundary of the marsh, 4 km (2 ½ miles) of forest trail have been built along the lower slopes of the U.B.C. Research Forest, affording views of the marsh and polder from roofed lookouts along the way. Bald eagles can often be seen soaring between forest and marsh, and, if you are lucky, a sandhill crane might alight beside the ditch. A few pairs of these stately birds breed in the sanctuary, in an area closed off at nesting season to protect them. Swallows make their nests in the tower, and in summer your long-range observations may be interrupted by their sleek bodies flashing past the lens of your binoculars.

Beavers and muskrats are present in the marsh, and though they are not often seen by daytime visitors, it is worth keeping your eye on the lodges near the observation tower. While dawdling there one afternoon in late September, I watched a family of beavers swimming outside a lodge. They propelled themselves with astonishing speed and seemed to be playing tag among the reeds. The beaver is wonderfully equipped for its aquatic life with dense, waterproofed fur which the animal oils and grooms with a special split claw. Flaps over its ears and nostrils, and transparent goggles over its eyes, enable the beaver to stay underwater for ten to fifteen minutes; a hard, flat tail serves as rudder, alarm device and brace for standing. The strong, yellow teeth that can topple a mature cottonwood tree grow as fast as they are worn down.

As you set off westward along the old treed dyke for the final leg of your walk, you'll see that many trees have been protected with wire to deter industrious beavers; others have already been felled according to the dam builders' plans. These plans, while sometimes conflicting with human purposes, are admirable: to build a dam to raise the water level; to build a safe house in which to raise young and stockpile food for the winter. Abandoned beaver ponds are not the devastated places they appear to be, for in time the old dam weakens and the pond drains, leaving a bed of rich silt that nurtures plants and saplings, and a new forest is begun. The beaver eats twigs, bark and leaves from the trees it cuts, transporting them to its lodge along tracks and channels through the vegetation, runways you might notice as you walk along the dyke.

The thickets of this wooded dyke are a haven for songbirds, and in summer there is a constant twittering as warblers, orioles, wrens, chickadees and nuthatches forage among the bushes. Keen bird-watchers visit the dyke for a sighting of the rarer least flycatcher or the gray catbird, which imitates the songs of others as well as producing its own mewing call. Keep an eye out for this slate-grey bird, almost the size of a robin, with a black cap and chestnut patch beneath its jauntily held tail.

Progress along this old dyke can be slow, with much to see and hear, but eventually you step out onto the road opposite the parking lot at Grant Narrows. Other dykes on the marsh and riverbank wait to be explored on other days.

HOW TO GET THERE: From Highway 7 (Lougheed Highway), turn left (east) on Dewdney Trunk Road just east of the Pitt River bridge. Go north at the junction with Harris Road, right on McNeil, and left on Rannie Road to its end at Grant Narrows. Journey time: 1 ¼ hours.

14
Kanaka Creek

HIGHLIGHTS
Woodland and canyon; waterfalls, sculptured sandstone; maidenhair ferns, foamflower; American dipper; tailed frogs

SEASON
All year

ROUND TRIP
2 km (1 ¼ miles)

TERRAIN
Some ups and downs. Good woodland paths and equestrian trails.

FAMILY WALK
There is a beautiful picnic area at Cliff Falls, but take care of small children around canyon edge.

FROM ITS BEGINNINGS on Blue Mountain, this typical west-coast stream gathers force as it tumbles down the forested slopes to carve its way between sandstone cliffs and plunge into a deep canyon. Then, playfulness over, it wanders through farmland and marsh to lose itself in the Fraser River. At present, much of the 12-km (7-mile) waterway is closed to the public, but it is intended that the creek be preserved as a linear park, with a trail linking Riverfront Park at the estuary to Cliff Falls and the existing Blue Mountain trail system.

To see Kanaka Creek at its liveliest you should go in spring or after heavy rainfall, when white water cascades over the rocky ledges and dances among the holes and fissures. But the summer visitor is rewarded too, for when the flow has subsided, the sculptured bedrock of the river is exposed, bearing witness to the work of centuries of rolling boulders pounding into the soft sandstone. Coal seams occur in the walls of the canyon, and fossil beds indicate that this region once basked in a tropical climate. Almost as surprising is the record that some

Hawaiian islanders were among early settlers in this area. Arriving as sailors on the Hudson's Bay Company's trading ships, many remained to work at the original Fort Langley, eventually buying land for themselves on the north side of the river. They were known as "kanakas."

The path to Cliff Falls runs along the bottom of the sports field, then descends through the woods to a bridge over the North Fork. A trail to the right, immediately before the bridge, leads to a view of the waterfall framed by the mossy limbs of surrounding trees. From the bridge you will see that the sheer walls of the canyon are clothed with vegetation, a stunning sight in summer when fronds of delicate maidenhair fern are massed against the black rock, with here and there the thin white flowers of goatsbeard dangling in space.

Maidenhair fern is deciduous, the dull green fronds springing up each year on moist, shady stream banks and cliffs, often in the spray zone of waterfalls. Farther along on your walk you may have an opportunity to examine the fern more closely, when you'll see that the pinnules, or lobes, of each frond have a ragged upper margin. Beneath the edges of this in-rolled fringe are the sori—the cases that hold the spores. Ferns are less advanced than flowering plants in that they do not produce seeds but reproduce by means of spores. The spores, provided they land in a moist place, germinate into unusual plants that resemble liverworts. These oddities in turn produce eggs and sperm, and only after fertilization takes place does the egg develop into a new fern.

For the best view of the sandstone bowls and ledges, walk along the bottom of the grassy slope and down a few steps to a viewpoint overlooking the main stream, Kanaka Creek. Below you, the water finds its way down chutes and channels to collect in a deep pool before sliding, or sometimes leaping, over the edge to embrace the North Fork tributary a few metres lower down. Continuing upstream to cross the Kanaka Creek bridge, you look out over a moonscape of smooth rock dimpled with craters.

The path climbs away from the creek on the east side, soon bringing you to the beginning of Canyon Trail, along which you head left. After crossing a minor stream, you find yourself walking through mixed woodland with a herb layer of sword fern and, throughout the summer, an airy, shimmering sea of *Tiarella*, or foamflower. Descending to a bend in the trail, you pass between two lengths of a massive nurse log. This great cedar, a deadfall, has been host for decades to generations of plants and wildlife. A section of the log has been cleared to expose the tree's growth rings, but time and weather are steadily erasing the record.

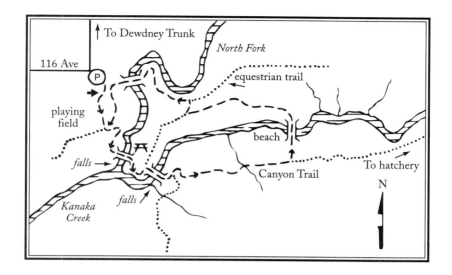

Moving on, you gain a little height with the help of some steps and enter a stand of tall, straight cedars and hemlocks with here and there a Douglas fir among them, all reaching for the light. And then it is time to part company with Canyon Trail, which carries on for a further 0.8 m (½ mile) to the Bell Irving fish hatchery, worth a separate visit sometime for a free tour of the rearing troughs and ponds. The hatchery can also be reached by car from 256th Street. For now, go left at the trail junction, following the sign to North Fork Loop Trail. A short descent brings you to an unusual suspension bridge over Kanaka Creek, approached from a curved ramp. Anyone with an interest in engineering will want to take a look at the bridge from below, but another good reason for taking the little path that leads down through the bushes at the foot of the ramp is to sit for a while on the beach and observe the creek at close quarters.

Here is where, in summer, you can examine the fronds of maidenhair fern sprouting from the rock wall and see how its dainty, fragile appearance is belied by the tough, purplish-black stalks. Looking upward, you might have an intriguing view of the white flowers or red berries of twistedstalk, which also finds a foothold on the cliff. Rocks, sand and pebbles make up the beach, past which the clear water flows via pools, glides and riffles. If you sit quietly at the edge of the stream for a while, where flotillas of water striders row themselves jerkily about on the surface, you may be joined by a chunky grey bird with a short tail and bill and a habit of bobbing and curtseying as it stands upon a rock in the

Suspension bridge over Kanaka Creek

stream. This is the dipper, unique among birds. Flying in short, fussy bursts close to the water, the dipper is able to dive and swim—though it does not have webbed toes—and walk on the stream bottom in its search for aquatic invertebrates and insect larvae. The dipper's nonstop bobbing habit is explained by science as a movement that enables the bird to see things rapidly from different angles. Science may have an explanation for the dipper's melodious song, offered up rain or shine, but I prefer to believe this endearing bird simply sings with pleasure at being near fast-flowing water.

Kanaka Creek boasts another unique resident—the tailed frog. This delicate-looking, brownish frog is likely to be hiding beneath a rock at the water's edge in the daytime, emerging at night to feed. As well as the male's tail-like appendage, an identifying feature is the frog's vertical, diamond-shaped pupils. Rather smaller than our pond frogs, this primitive little creature is an inhabitant of mountain streams and forests.

When it is time to leave the beach, a short climb awaits you before the trail becomes a smooth, level track through alder woods to a barrier and junction. Follow signs for North Fork Loop Trail, right and then left. The creek is audible below as you descend on a winding equestrian trail. (Please remember that horses, though large, are easily startled by sudden sounds or movements.) After passing by some large nurse logs, you come to your last bridge, back across the North Fork, flowing more quietly here over its boulder-strewn bed and flat slabs of rock. Thereafter, the trail climbs gently through the woods to intersect your original route down to Cliff Falls. Turn right, and you are soon strolling back past the hazelnut and blackberry bushes bordering the sports field to your car.

HOW TO GET THERE: From the Dewdney Trunk Road in Maple Ridge, turn south on 252nd Street and drive to the end of the road to the Cliff Falls parking lot next to the sports field. Journey time: 1 ¼ hours.

15
Spirea Trail

GOLDEN EARS PROVINCIAL PARK
MAPLE RIDGE

HIGHLIGHTS
Forest and bog; Alouette Lake; sundew, Indian pipe, fungi, mosses; amphibians

SEASON
March to November

ROUND TRIP
2.4 km (1½ miles)

TERRAIN
Ups and downs. Forest trail and boardwalk.

FAMILY WALK
There is a picnic area and swimming beach at the south end of Alouette Lake, adjacent to the day-use parking lot.

IF THE MENTION of Golden Ears conjures up a picture of rugged trails to lofty summits, you will not be mistaken. The rampart of jagged peaks that catches the evening sun 50 km (30 miles) east of Vancouver does indeed provide some strenuous climbing for the adventurous hiker, and the northern reaches of the park are a mountain wilderness extending to the boundary of Garibaldi Provincial Park, between Squamish and Whistler. But the southern end of Golden Ears Park lies more sedately in the Alouette Valley, where less ambitious walkers can explore forest and creekside trails, such as the easy walk to Lower Falls, or the fascinating Spirea Nature Trail suggested here.

The lake and its surrounding forests were for hundreds of years favourite fishing and hunting grounds of the Coast Salish Indians. Later, giant trees fell to the axe and saw in a ten-year railway-logging operation that ended abruptly in 1931, when fire swept through the valley. Reminders of both disturbances are evident today in the fire-blackened stumps and snags, remnants of the old railroads and pieces of

Orange lacteria

rusting steel cable and machinery, all gradually being covered by the vigorous second growth of western hemlocks and cedars.

To follow the first few hundred metres of Spirea Trail from parking lot 2 may require diligence. Start from the south end of the parking lot and walk down the gravel track heading left from the access road. A few metres along, a Spirea Trail sign on the right indicates the beginning of the trail, though it may be bushy and difficult to see. Almost immediately, this path crosses a gravel equestrian trail (there is a map at this

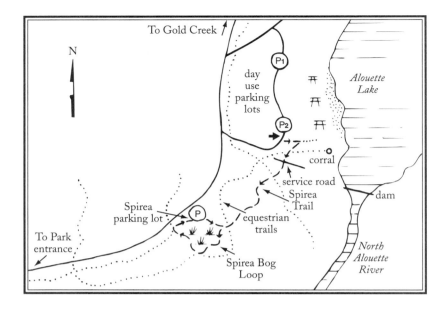

point) and descends to a bridge over a creek, from where it proceeds briefly through the woods to meet a service road. Cross this, enter the forest on the opposite side, and you are safely on your way.

Deciduous trees and salmonberry bushes are soon replaced by an evergreen forest where buttressed cedar stumps and burnt snags stand mutely among the ferns and foamflower. As you wend your way up and down the slopes on the needle-covered path, you'll see many beautiful mosses layered over the forest floor and debris. As well as a hand lens, the serious study of mosses requires a head for long Latin names; however, some of the most common mosses have acquired descriptive English names (often more than one) that help us to distinguish one from another. Fern moss is easy to recognize, with its arching fernlike branches that advance over the ground in steps with each year's new growth. Fallen logs may be covered with dense mats of shaggy (or lanky or pipecleaner) moss, its branched stems bearing tiny leaves that twist and curl. An erect moss with unusually large, oval leaves often found in damp spots and on rotting logs generally goes by the name of fan moss, or large leafy moss. Like fungi, mosses help to break down organic material into new soil. They also help to check soil erosion and act as a reservoir by retaining moisture.

After gaining some height, you descend past a connecting trail on the right, through a stand of hemlocks affected by the mistletoe parasite, and cross another equestrian trail. A few steps farther and you find yourself in the midst of a dark, enchanted forest, where the trees rise straight and tall from an emerald carpet studded with fairy toadstools and ghostly white Indian pipe. There could be trolls.

Toadstools seem to have a questionable existence in the fungi world. The dictionary defines a toadstool as "an umbrella-shaped fungus" and a mushroom as "an edible kind of fungus." Some mycologists go along with this, while others refer cautiously to "so-called toadstools." Some ignore toadstools altogether and stick with poisonous and nonpoisonous mushrooms. The question was settled for me in the Spirea forest when I bent to examine a cluster of purplish fungi and a warty brown toad hopped away from my foot.

The toad turned itself into a leaf while I searched for it, materializing only to disappear, backwards I'm sure, beneath a log. Our western toad is quite adapted for life on land and may stray quite a distance from water during the nonbreeding season. It can be brown, green or blackish, with spotted underparts and a white stripe down its back. Its golden eyes have horizontal pupils. The reddish warts on the toad's back and legs are poison glands, and when cornered, the creature will rear up onto all fours and puff itself out, the better to display its warts to the attacker. Only the garter snake is not deterred by the foul-tasting fluid toads secrete. The toad is active at night, feeding on worms and slugs, and probably frequents toadstools not as a seat but for the insects and slugs they attract.

In spring, toads converge upon the ponds to breed. Unike bullfrogs, male toads have no mating call to beckon their females but must roam the pond, clasping other amphibians, or even branches, until they happen upon a suitable partner. Thousands of eggs are laid in long strings among the pond vegetation. In the absence of further parental care, the little black tadpoles fend for themselves by banding together and swimming around the pond in synchronized formations. In six to eight weeks they mature into toadlets and go their separate ways.

When you come within sight of the Spirea parking lot and other facilities, your route joins the interpretive loop trail around a remnant of sphagnum bog. Numbered stops tie in with a park leaflet and panels explain the natural history of the bog. From boardwalks over the ponds you will be able to see the mounds of sphagnum mosses that create and support this particular kind of wetland. Living mosses are layered over decaying ones, forming a blanket of peat that effectively blocks circulation and drainage. The stagnant water becomes acidic from the decaying material and loses most of its oxygen, so that bog plants must be able to survive with few nutrients. Most are evergreens that can hold onto their leaves, and therefore their nutrients, for several years. Some, like Labrador tea and swamp laurel, have leathery, inwardly rolled leaves lined with hairs that help to conserve moisture. Other plants make up for the deficiency of nitrogen by becoming carnivorous.

One of these is sundew, a bog plant with little chlorophyll that supplements its diet by catching insects. Its round leaves, growing in a basal rosette, are fringed with hairs and knobbed tentacles that exude sticky drops. When a fly or mosquito becomes caught in this substance, the leaf's outer fringe of hairs slowly closes inward to hold the victim firmly in the trap. Enzymes are released to begin digestion of the insect's proteins. The white sundew flowers, coiled around one side of the stem, are sparse and elusive, opening only in midday sunshine. The plant is difficult to spot among the other vegetation, though sometimes the sparkle of its sticky drops catches the eye.

At the end of the boardwalk comes another stretch of forest, opening out to a second patch of bog where there is little open water. Shrubs, even cedar and hemlock seedlings, are gaining a foothold here. Hardhack, the spirea that lends its name to the trail, grows profusely on the fringes, sending up its fluffy pink flowers in summer.

Continue through the trees until yet another equestrian trail crosses your path. Turn right on this, and right again in a few metres on the Spirea loop trail running parallel to the road. This narrow path, between hedges of spirea, passes alongside a dark pond before entering a belt of trees. A final stretch of boardwalk brings you back to the Spirea parking area and the end of the interpretive loop. Head to the right, past the outhouses, to rejoin the trail from the day-use parking, along which you retrace your steps through the enchanted forest.

On your next visit to Golden Ears Park, you might like to explore the Tiarella Nature Trail or the trail and boardwalks around Mike Lake. These walks are shown on the park leaflet, available at the various information stands.

HOW TO GET THERE: From Highway 7 in Haney, follow signs north to Golden Ears Park. Drive 7 km (4½ miles) beyond the park entrance to a road signed "Boat Rental" (the first turning on the right after the Spirea Nature Trail parking lot), which leads to the south end of the day-use parking lot 2. Park here. Journey time: 1½ hours.

16
Rolley Lake

ROLLEY LAKE PROVINCIAL PARK
MISSION

HIGHLIGHTS
Lake, evergreen forest, swamp; sweet gale, ninebark; banana slugs

SEASON
All year

ROUND TRIP
2.8 km (1 ¾ miles)

TERRAIN
Flat. Boardwalk and forest trail. Some areas accessible to wheelchairs.

FAMILY WALK
There are picnic tables at the day-use beach, also a campground with 65 sites on the northeast side of the lake. There is excellent fishing, but no motors are allowed.

FOR A FAMILY OUTING in the region around the Stave dams, it is hard to beat a visit to Rolley Lake. Tucked away amid tall trees on a plateau above Stave Lake, Rolley is secluded yet welcoming, attributes that perhaps led homesteaders James and Fanny Rolley to settle there in the 1880s. Today, thoughtfully planned campgrounds and a ban on motor boats help to preserve a peaceful atmosphere, with no sounds other than birdsong and the voices of people enjoying themselves in small boats on the water. The lake is 1.5 km (1 mile) in length, so a complete circuit is within most people's ability. All of the trail is well maintained, but those with wheelchairs should use the path along the northeast shore of the lake. Others can make a clockwise circuit from the day-use beach and parking lot.

Follow the Lakeside Trail sign past the outhouses and avenue of picnic tables until you find yourself descending on what was once a corduroy logging road built to carry out the giant western red cedars and Douglas firs of a hundred years ago. Arriving at the lakeshore, you venture upon a long boardwalk across a richly vegetated, swampy meadow. Seeking their way through the shrubs and reeds, several gurgling streams feed into the lake; birds and insects dart among the bushes. At first it seems an overwhelming task to identify any of the lush, tangled growth, but in summer you might notice the yellowish, wax-coated cones of sweet gale, a species of myrtle. Sweet gale is a rarity, or at least not often spotted among stands of hardhack, which it resembles, but along the shores of Rolley Lake it appears to dominate, and no doubt plays a valuable role in the wetland community.

Usually, plants get needed nitrogen from the soil, but in poor soil conditions certain plants, such as sweet gale, are able to use atmospheric nitrogen by means of bacteria harboured in nodules on their roots, thus helping to maintain the fertility of the soil for the benefit of the plant community. Sweet gale is deciduous, producing greenish-yellow catkins before its leaves appear in spring and keeping its brown cones of seeds through the winter. Its aromatic leaves are lance-shaped, dotted with yellow wax glands above and below.

The boardwalk widens into a platform from which you can study the marsh plants and the aquatics at the water's peaty edge, and gaze down the length of the lake to the forested hills beyond. Water parsley and marsh cinquefoil can be found in summer, and skunk cabbage announces its presence at most seasons. Arriving at the end of the boardwalk, you step quite suddenly onto a soft path entering the forest.

Staying on the main trail (minor paths wander off into the woods or down to the lakeshore), you soon come to a bridge across a wide inlet creek, a pretty spot in May and June when the overhanging ninebark bushes are dappled with white flower heads. These turn into bunches of rough, reddish seed husks that last through the summer until the seeds are ripe. Ninebark loves streamsides and damp meadow openings, where it can spread its arching branches and grow to 3 or 4 metres (10–13 feet) in height. There are supposedly nine layers of shreddy bark on the main stem, hence its name.

The forest slopes steeply down to the western shore of the lake, usually with an understorey of vine maple, red alder, salmonberry and deer fern, but in some places the tall, straight conifers crowd together to make a closed-canopy forest bare of undergrowth and deliciously cool on a hot day. Several paths lead down to the water, some to jetties and fishing spots. Exploring along the shore, you will find more sweet gale shrubs and rafts of floating-leaved pondweed in the water. Huckleberry is prevalent in the more open edges of the forest. So is false azalea, with

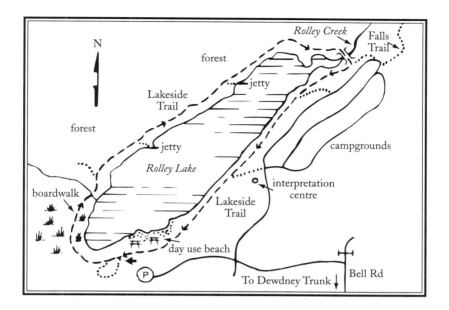

its pinkish bell-shaped flowers drooping from their long stems among whorls of blueish-green leaves. Fool's huckleberry is another name for this shrub, because its disappointingly dry berries are inedible.

It is likely that along damper stretches of the trail you have been stepping, with a shudder, around some interesting wildlife. Our native forest slug, or banana slug as we call this yellowish-green mollusk, is not much loved. Even the dictionary definition of a slug as "a shell-less snail destructive to small plants" is prejudiced, for here in the forest the slug is an efficient and necessary clean-up agent, willing to eat leaves, fruit, fungi and animal droppings. The banana slug is largely a nocturnal diner, but sometimes crawls out in the daytime to tidy something up, oblivious to danger from hiking boots. Tentacles waving—its primitive eyes, located on the ends, are sensitive to light but cannot form images—the slug secretes a trail of slime to crawl over and is capable of travelling up the trunks of trees as well as over the ground. A breathing hole on the animal's right side, near the head, acts as a rudimentary lung, allowing air to pass in and out, and the possession of both male and female organs enables all slugs to lay eggs.

Approaching the northern end of the lake, you will pass many large stumps and nurse logs, some moss-covered, others dry and corky. Two more inlet streams are crossed, after which the trail enters a dark, shady stretch of forest. Any children in your party will be sure to spot the old

stump on the left, complete with sawyer's notches for eyes and, thanks to someone's imagination, nose and mouth as well, so that its cheerful face smiles out of the gloom. The path veers away from the lakeshore briefly before arriving at the bridge over the outlet stream, Rolley Creek. This is a good place to lean on the rail for a while, watching waxwings searching for berries among the creekside trees. A shattering call and a flash of blue announces the Steller's jay, swooping down from the cedar boughs or taking a break from raiding the nearby campsites.

If a straightforward return along the eastern shore of the lake is not enough for you, there is another option. From the T junction above the bridge, you can head left, then left again on the signposted Falls Trail. Through hemlocks and huckleberry bushes a path descends, quite steeply at the end, to Rolley Creek falls, where the water drops over a broad ledge to continue in a more unruly fashion down the steep hillside towards Stave Lake. Allow a half-hour to visit the falls and return to the Rolley Lake trail. If you include the 1350-m (¾-mile) Mission Forest Service loop trail, you will be tackling a minor hike with some steep slopes.

By turning right at the junction above the Rolley Creek bridge, you are on your way back to the beach and parking lot via a wide, well-manicured trail that closely follows the lakeshore. From an avenue of young hemlocks and cedars, the path opens out into a small, somewhat muddy beach. The lake is deepest at this end, close to 30 metres (100 feet), and you may well see one of Rolley Lake's famous rainbow trout break the surface in pursuit of an unlucky insect. Side paths through the trees lead to the secluded campsites and an interpretive centre for visitors. After a few minutes of walking, the day-use beach, with its grassy field and inviting picnic tables, comes into sight.

HOW TO GET THERE: Drive approximately 14 km (9 miles) east from Maple Ridge along the Dewdney Trunk Road. Turn left (north) on Bell Road and follow signs to Rolley Lake Provincial Park. Journey time: 1½ hours.

FACING PAGE: *Sweet gale*

17
Serpentine River Trails

TYNEHEAD REGIONAL PARK
SURREY

HIGHLIGHTS
Forest, meadows and river; Sitka spruce, nurse logs; wildflowers; bush-tits; butterflies

SEASON
All year

ROUND TRIP
3.7 km (2 ¼ miles)

TERRAIN
Gentle slopes. Woodland and field paths. One section accessible to wheelchairs.

FAMILY WALK
There are picnic tables at the hatchery parking lot and at Serpentine Hollow, which is also furnished with a butterfly garden and a tree-hugging viewing platform.

A WALK IN THE COUNTRY best describes what this peaceful park in the heart of North Surrey has to offer. Trails follow the winding Serpentine River through meadows and woodland, beneath tall conifers and past remnants of old orchards. The park is a haven for small mammals, birds and the trout and salmon fry reared at the Tynehead Hatchery. Several entrances to the park offer a choice of itinerary to suit both energetic walkers and leisurely strollers. I have described a fairly comprehensive circuit, but you will see from the map that it lends itself to division. In any case, the park is just as enjoyable for winter walks as for summer rambles, and you will want to visit more than once. Nature lovers with wheelchairs can explore the trail starting from the hatchery parking lot, stopping at an observation platform overlooking the river, before crossing an elegant arched bridge to incorporate a 500-metre interpretive loop trail.

Walkers follow the same path to the bridge, but leaving the interpretive loop for their return, continue along the east side of the river through mixed forest with occasional cherry trees and hawthorn bushes bordering the trail. Hawthorn is prevalent in the park, sometimes growing in dense thickets. On a day in early spring, when the hawthorns were bare of leaves, I spotted a bushtit's nest hanging from the thorny branches and went for a closer look. What a marvel of architecture it was—a 20-cm (8-inch)–long socklike pocket woven around the twigs, the entrance a tiny hole on the side, near the top. Small wonder that it takes both male and female a month or more to construct such a home from grasses, leaves, lichens and spiders' webs, then carefully line it with hair and feathers and downy material collected from plants. In this snug dwelling, both birds incubate and turn their eggs, staying together in the nest at night.

Bushtits are a western bird, cousins of our chickadees. They are tiny creatures, noticeable only because they feed in flocks. The lively, twittering bands flit from bush to bush, examining the twigs from all sides, even upside down, for their diet of aphids and beetles, before moving on with one accord to the next bush or tree. Should you get the chance to observe one of these restless mites for a moment, you will see a fluffy, grey and brown bird with a long tail and stubby bill. Their round, bright eyes, yellow in the females, give the little creatures a surprisingly imperious aspect. Thickets and streamsides are their favourite habitat, so you will see plenty in the park, especially during winter.

After a few minutes of walking from the arched bridge below the hatchery, you will arrive at the edge of a meadow, where the Serpentine Loop trail is joined on the right by the access trail from the 168th Street entrance. Passing a section of wooden fence at the edge of the meadow, you reenter the forest. Many large conifers and broadleaf maples remain in this area, towering above the lower layer of birch, alder and vine maple. In spring, the ground is carpeted with false lily-of-the-valley, bleeding heart and yellow violets, with occasional patches of trillium to gladden the eye. Massive stumps attest to the kind of forest early settlers found here a hundred years ago.

You will cross several feeder streams on this section of the trail. These may be dry in summer, but in early spring the woods are lively with their chatter. Towhees forage busily in the undergrowth, bushtits and chestnut-backed chickadees work their way among the branches overhead, and the winter wren sings its long song.

When you come to a path forking right, signposted to Serpentine

Hollow picnic area, you must make a decision. The Serpentine River Loop trail you are on leads down by way of a long boardwalk to a bridge across the river, and thence back to the hatchery bridge along the opposite bank. Let us say you decide to incorporate the Serpentine Hollow in your walk. Before heading off to the right along the bottom of the field, take a few minutes to follow the boardwalk down to the river. Here, close to the beginning of its 27-km (17-mile) journey to the ocean at Mud Bay, the Serpentine runs clear and shallow. It is home to chum, coho and chinook salmon and to steelhead, cutthroat and rainbow trout, mostly reared at the Tynehead Hatchery.

After backtracking to the junction, your route soon leaves the field to enter a tangled woodland of moss-covered vine maples amid boggy patches of skunk cabbage. Immediately after crossing a hump-backed bridge, you will see a very large Sitka spruce on your left. This species of spruce is common throughout the park, being a tree of lower elevations, at home on a mossy, ferny forest floor. This specimen has a long trunk devoid of lower branches, its distinctive scaly bark disguised by moss, but elsewhere in the park you will see large spruce with sweeping, horizontal branches along their length, from which the needle leaves hang in feathery fronds—a deceptive daintiness, you'll discover, when you feel the sharp, stiff needles that bristle all around the twigs. Aboriginal people believed the sharp needles gave the tree protection from evil thoughts, but alas, many are turned into pulp wood every day. Haida and Tlingit Indians were more restrained in their harvesting, taking only pieces of the roots to weave into hats and baskets, or using the softened pitch for waterproofing. In spring the red pollen cones at the ends of the twigs will catch your eye. Cylindrical seed cones, about 7 cm (3 inches) long with wavy, reddish-brown scales, are usually plentiful on the ground around the tree.

A flight of wooden steps brings you to Serpentine Hollow. Turn left to sample its delights. (The trail to the right leads to the 161st Street entrance and parking area.) Picnic tables are set among the trees in the grassy space beside the river; a bench overlooking a planted butterfly garden invites you to contemplate this attraction, and if you are visiting on a fine summer day you may see tiger swallowtails, red admirals, blues and whites sipping nectar from their favourite flowers.

The park's meadows and woodland fringes are also attractive to butterflies, providing both food plants for the larvae and flowers for the adults. We all remember learning during our early school days about the four stages of a butterfly's life—egg, caterpillar, pupa, butterfly—but

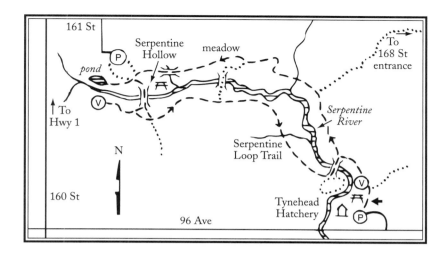

hundreds of years ago caterpillars were believed to have come from the dew that formed on leaves overnight. It was a notion hardly more fanciful than the scientific facts we now know: from an egg glued to the underside of a leaf—aspen or cottonwood for the swallowtail, thistle for the painted lady—hatches a caterpillar that eats its way through the chosen leaves, periodically shedding its skin until overtaken by torpidity, whereupon it weaves a pad of silk to hold onto and a silken girdle for support and encases itself in a shroud that it later rends open to emerge as a fully developed insect with wondrously patterned wings.

Butterflies and moths belong to the order of insects called lepidoptera, from the Greek "lepidos" meaning scaly, and "ptera" meaning wings, and it is these tiny scales—about 125,000 per square inch—that create the colour patterns. One of the best ways to examine a butterfly is to catch it napping. They do rest, sometimes upon a flower, sometimes beneath a leaf, and they also need to bask frequently to warm themselves for flying. The eyes of moths and butterflies are always open, but they are not always seeing eyes. Butterflies are shortsighted but, unlike us, they have the ability to see ultraviolet colours. As these colours are present both in their own wings and in many of the flowers they visit, they may guide the insects to a mate or to a source of food. To fool the birds, who are only too pleased to snatch a butterfly snack, the insect has several devices: tails disguised as heads, painted eyespots that startle and confuse. Some have a bad taste, guaranteed to put a bird off for life, while others that taste good to predators protect themselves by closely resembling their unpalatable relatives.

As well as food plants for several species, the butterfly garden by the Serpentine has water and, at most seasons, a damp or muddy patch of ground. Here you might see a congregation of swallowtails engaged in "puddling," an activity common to many kinds of butterflies, in which they extract salt and minerals not found in the plants they feed on but needed by the males for procreation. There is more to a butterfly's life than sailing from flower to flower on a summer day.

Beyond the garden is a small pond used by the Tynehead Hatchery for overwintering salmon and trout fry. Overlooking it you will spot a platform built around a large hemlock on the slope above. This is reached by climbing the Trillium Trail on the other side of the river, a side trip that affords a bird's-eye view of Serpentine Hollow.

On the south side of the river, a sign directing you to the Serpentine River Loop Trail is the beginning of your return journey. You will walk beneath lofty evergreens and among many wonderful examples of nurse logs and stumps. A trail to the left leads to the bridge you visited earlier, but your homeward route now stays south of the river until you arrive back at the hatchery bridge where your circuit began. All that is left to explore is the short interpretive loop with its riverbank viewpoints before you head back up the path to your car.

HOW TO GET THERE: From Highway 1, east of the Port Mann bridge, take the 160th Street exit 50. Turn left on 104th Avenue, right on 160th Street. In 1.6 km (1 mile), turn left on 96th Avenue and proceed for a further 1.6 km (1 mile) to the park entrance at the Tynehead Hatchery. Journey time: 45 minutes.

FACING PAGE: *Conifer with cattail moss*

18
Blackie Spit

CRESCENT BEACH
SURREY

HIGHLIGHTS
Sandspit, tidal marsh, saltwater bay, dunes; dune plants; waterfowl, shorebirds, raptors; harbour seals

SEASON
All year. Fall and winter best for bird-watching.

ROUND TRIP
Up to 3.5 km (2 miles)

TERRAIN
Flat. Paths and tracks, wet in places.

FAMILY WALK
A trip to Blackie Spit can be combined with a walk along the promenade to Crescent Beach village or time spent on the beach.

THE WINDING SERPENTINE and Nicomekl rivers slide into the shallow northeastern part of Boundary Bay, helping to form the estuarine delta known as Mud Bay. This large area of mudflats, bathed daily by the tides, provides food and refuge for thousands of waterfowl and shorebirds, both resident and migratory. Jutting into Mud Bay like a crooked finger is Blackie Spit, an excellent viewing spot for the open bay and adjacent tidal marshes. Named after Walter Blackie, who in the 1870s farmed the land now occupied by the village of Crescent Beach, the sandspit was once the site of an Indian village. Archaeological digging has turned up evidence of shellfish gathered by Coast Salish people 8000 years ago.

Be sure to take binoculars on this outing. Rare birds are sometimes sighted in Mud Bay, especially after an autumnal storm when migrating birds get blown off course and seek a haven to wait out the weather. Fall is a good time to visit Blackie Spit, in any case. Try to be there when the tide is fairly high, otherwise shorebirds will be too far out on

Mudflats

the mudflats to be properly observed, even with binoculars. Dress warmly—the sandspit can be a breezy place.

Follow the gravel road north from the parking lot, go through the gate, and walk out first of all along the seaward side of the spit. The beach is a mixture of sand and shells, looped with tidal necklaces of weed and debris. You will probably see loons and grebes diving offshore or rolling onto one side in the water to groom their feathers. In fall and winter, the exquisitely patterned loon depicted on our dollar coin is dressed in greyish brown, its distinctive, checkered back feathers pale and muted. The loon is a powerful diver, sometimes descending to a depth of 60 metres (195 feet), and able to stay underwater for two or three minutes, where it swims rapidly in pursuit of its prey; small fish are sometimes consumed underwater. After wintering on the sea coast, loons move to inland lakes to breed, one pair of birds often laying claim to an entire lake. During courtship, the air resounds with their haunting cries, likened to wolf wails or mad laughter.

If you spot chunky black ducks bobbing about in the bay, they could be surf scoters. A close look through your binoculars will show the male's white head and neck patches and large, colourful bill. This stout black, white and orange tool, swollen at the base, is used to poke out clams and to prise mussels off rocks. Surf scoters are diving ducks, often seen living up to their name in rough, open water, where they congregate in rafts, diving and reforming with military precision. They are common in Boundary Bay in winter, departing in spring for breeding grounds in Alaska and northern Canada.

On the sheltered inland side of the spit, a mixed company of ducks dabbles in the shallows, a tapestry of feathered backs, punctuated by herons. Flocks of shorebirds blow in like leaves in the wind to probe the mudflats for worms and crustaceans. In September, some yellowlegs and dowitchers may still be around, and a lucky fall sighting would be that of a long-billed curlew working its way along the freshly exposed mud with its amazingly long, downward-curved bill.

By September, the beds of glasswort on the sandspit are turning a rosy purplish-brown. You will still see gumweed, dune tansy and the dusky, filigreed leaves of silver burweed as you walk back up the sandspit. Keep to the east side and follow the path between the asters, goldenrod and blackberry bushes around the end of the bay. If it is not too wet, you can walk beside the fence bordering the tidal pond and continue on a path along the shore for a close look at the channels and mudflats. Otherwise, stay with the main trail as it opens out into a meadow and dunes on the north side of Farm Slough.

The many pilings around the mouth of this backwater of the Nicomekl River are remnants of the Olympic Oyster Company that operated there around 1911. Today the pilings are favourite perching posts of gulls and cormorants. Clumps of black-eyed Susans—perhaps garden escapes, but delightful to come across nonetheless—flourish in the dunes well into October, some with deep red petals merging into yellow at the tips, and knobby purple seedheads.

The trail continues around the end of the slough, between tall stalks of tansy and goldenrod, to merge with a gravel path. Go left again in a few metres on the narrow trail along the southern bank, a stretch that ought to be named Snowberry Lane. Benches along the way are well placed for viewing the sleepy, mud-filled slough, and are convenient for observing songbirds that frequent the alder, birch and crabapple trees of the wooded dyke. After passing through a thicket of wild rose bushes, the trail rejoins the gravel path in front of a white gate. Go through the gate onto the promontory of land on the left.

From here you have a good view of the oyster pilings and the expanse of Mud Bay beyond, with the slender supports of the Alex Fraser bridge

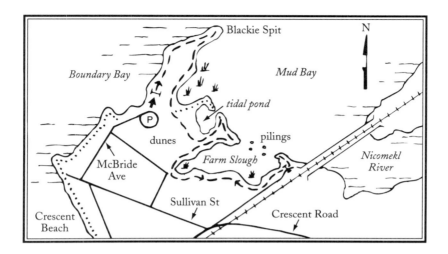

and the tall buildings around Central Park crowning the picture. Swing your binoculars around past the nearby boatyard to the Nicomekl River, disgorging its waters beneath the railway trestle, and scan the neighbouring islets for lounging harbour seals; this is a favourite place for them to haul out. Harbour seals are common along the British Columbia coast, often frequenting shallow bays and inlets, but also travelling far upstream in rivers to appear sometimes in inland lakes. Pups are born in May and June, usually on a secluded sandbar, and are able to swim at birth. The mothers guard their young devotedly, pulling them underwater when danger threatens, but many fall prey to killer whales, their natural enemy, or end their lives in commercial fishing nets while seeking their diet of fish and crustaceans.

You can return by the gravel path to the end of Farm Slough, or retrace your steps along the dyke and dune path to the parking lot. If you are spending time in Crescent Beach village, you might be able to pick up a bird checklist for Blackie Spit from the White Rock and Surrey Naturalists' information centre at the foot of Beecher Avenue. The centre is open on weekends from 1:00 to 5:00 p.m. October through May.

HOW TO GET THERE: From Highway 99 south, take the Crescent Beach turnoff. Follow Crescent Road for about 5 km (3 miles) and turn right on Sullivan Street, immediately after crossing the railway tracks. Go right again on McBride Avenue and continue to its end at a parking lot. Journey time: 1 hour. By bus: Take the No. 351 from Vancouver to Sullivan and McBride.

19
Reifel Bird Sanctuary

DELTA

HIGHLIGHTS
Marsh, slough and woodland; Westham Island; snow geese, sandhill cranes, ducks, shorebirds, raptors, songbirds

SEASON
All year. November to March for snow geese.

TERRAIN
Flat. Good paths and dykes, a limited area accessible to wheelchairs.

ROUND TRIP
3 km (2 miles)

FAMILY WALK
There are picnic tables outside the entrance, well attended by friendly ducks, geese and pigeons. Birdseed, bird checklists and books are available at the visitor centre. A museum housing a collection of stuffed birds is open at weekends.

ONCE OWNED AND FARMED by the George C. Reifel family, the northern tip of Westham Island, called Reifel Island, is now Crown land, reserved as a refuge for the thousands of migratory and nesting birds that frequent the Fraser River floodplain. The 340-ha (850-acre) refuge is managed by the B.C. Waterfowl Society and is open to the public daily from 9:00 a.m. to 4:00 p.m. The admission fee helps with the cost of maintaining the trails and providing other facilities for visitors. Dogs are not allowed in the sanctuary.

Because the bird population of the refuge changes with the seasons, it is useful to know what you might find at any time. The greatest number of migratory ducks, geese and swans can be seen in winter; raptors, too, are most common then. In spring, when many of the wintering birds move on to their northern nesting grounds, shorebirds pass through the sanctuary. By April and May resident birds will be busy nesting, duck-

Sandhill crane

lings and goslings appearing on the scene by June. Songbirds such as warblers and flycatchers will be present in summer, while others, including towhees, juncos, chickadees, wrens and sparrows, are permanent residents. In summer the marsh may seem quiet, as young waterfowl have not yet learned to fly and adults are going through their moulting period, during which they too are temporarily flightless and spend much time in hiding.

The tidal waterways of the marsh are controlled to accommodate this ever-changing population. Areas left dry in summer are flooded gradually in spring and fall for the incoming shorebirds, with maximum water in the ponds during winter for the ducks and geese.

The Fraser River estuary is a wintering ground for vast migratory flocks of lesser snow geese from Siberia. Arriving in late fall, up to 50,000 geese rest and feed offshore and in the fields and marshes of Westham Island, before returning to their arctic breeding grounds in spring. Smaller than a Canada goose, this white bird has black-tipped wings and a dark patch on the side of the bill. A field of feeding geese hums with muttering and gabbling sounds, with now and again a chorus of high-pitched "kowks" as a group lands or departs. When an entire flock takes flight, the air vibrates with wing beats and a shadow sweeps over the ground as they pass. Offshore, the flocks rise and settle like cresting waves as they forage along the seaward edge of the marsh at low tide.

Now to explore the network of trails. Be sure to take binoculars and dress warmly for a winter visit—Reifel Island can be cold and windy. The warming hut near the entrance offers a welcome retreat, with a wood stove, lunch table and photographs of avian inhabitants of the refuge. On first setting out, you may find you must run the gauntlet of expert panhandlers. Pigeons, mallards, gadwalls and other ducks have to be stepped over. Canada geese barge through the crush, eyes fixed on your bag of birdseed.

Farther along, near the information display, one or two pairs of exquisitely patterned wood ducks might be sitting atop the fence. These beautiful ducks, with their dashing swept-back crests, are swift and agile flyers, adept at dodging branches as they wing through the woods. They nest in hollow trees or in the boxes provided, the female lining her home with down plucked from her breast. Soon after hatching, the ducklings jump bravely from the nest at their mother's prompting and follow her to cover. By this time, the male wood duck has retired with his peers to secluded waterways to undergo his summer moult, an event endured by the males of all duck species. The rainbow feathers are shed and the flightless males remain in what is known as eclipse plumage until fall, when the handsome bridegroom plumage is restored, ready for the next breeding season. It is interesting to note that the species name for the wood duck is "*sponsa*," which is Latin for "betrothed." The females also undergo a moult in late summer but retain their dark brown colouring and distinctive white eye ring throughout.

A concealed viewing platform, or blind, in this area offers a view of

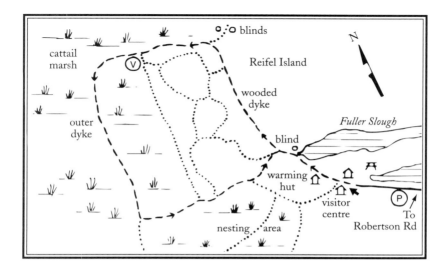

the freshwater slough on the east side of the refuge. Here you might see ducks and geese feeding beneath the bordering willows and crabapple boughs. Continuing northward along the wooded path—the evergreens were planted by early farmers as a windbreak—you become aware that chickadees, fox sparrows and other woodland birds are accompanying you, flitting from bush to bush in the expectation of a handout from your seed bag. Some are tame enough to feed from your hand.

A walk around the perimeter of the sanctuary takes you through a variety of bird habitats, but first you might wish to make a short diversion into the interior trails. In summer, these grassy, sheltered paths and ditches, bordered by blackberries and wild roses, are a haven for young songbirds and ducklings. Afterwards, head for the observation tower on the northern side of the refuge and continue along the outer dyke.

A vast cattail marsh now lies between you and the river mouth. Binoculars are essential here and will show you hawks and eagles quartering the marsh, red-winged blackbirds feeding among the cattails, and in winter perhaps a snowy owl resting on driftwood. Offshore, you might spot flocks of trumpeter swans and snow geese, detachments of the latter rising and forming into skeins as they return to the fields around the refuge.

On the inland side of the dyke, shovelers, widgeon, teal and pintails dabble in the shallow water, and sandpipers run to and fro along the flats. Bossy little coots scoot around the ponds, unintimidated by the larger birds. It is fascinating (provided the wind isn't sweeping across the marsh) to sit for a while and listen to the music: quacks, cheeps and whistles from the ponds, the harsh croak of a passing heron, the creaky call of the redwing, the honking of geese, the murmer of wings over-head. On one occasion, while indulging in this exercise, I realized my unfocussed eye was resting upon an uncommonly silent denizen of the marsh—a western painted turtle lay straddled upon a half-submerged branch enjoying the late September sunshine.

The southwest section of the outer dyke is reserved for nesting and is usually closed to the public. Either of the paths heading east between the ponds leads to the entrance and parking lot. As you head back, keep an eye out in this area for the resident pair of sandhill cranes. Westham Island is not a natural stopping-place for cranes, and this female was brought to the manager to be hand-raised. Later, the young male crane flew in to join her. For two seasons the pair have made a nest on the raft visible from the warming hut, but so far their eggs have been infertile. (An egg from 1995 can be seen in the shop.) Unlike the heron, these larger birds fly with neck oustretched; when they alight, a red forehead patch is noticeable. To come upon the cranes preening their buffy-grey feathers beside the pool would be a fitting finale to a walk around the sanctuary. But in any case, every visit to Reifel offers something new.

HOW TO GET THERE: The sanctuary is situated on Westham Island at the mouth of the Fraser River's south arm. Leave Highway 99 at the Victoria Ferry exit 28, then in 1.6 km (1 mile) head west on the Ladner Trunk Road (48th Avenue). Proceed through Ladner centre, jogging left on 47A Avenue, which becomes River Road West. In just under 3 km (2 miles), turn right onto the Westham Island bridge. Continue on Westham Island Road for almost 5 km (3 miles), where signs to the Reifel Bird Sanctuary direct you through a gate on your left. Journey time: 45 minutes.

20
Delta Nature Reserve

BURNS BOG
DELTA

HIGHLIGHTS
Sphagnum bog, bog forest; lodgepole pine, Pacific crabapple; Labrador tea, swamp laurel, sweet gale; fungi

SEASON
All year

ROUND TRIP
2.8 km (1 ¾ miles)

TERRAIN
Flat. Boardwalk, trail and service road.

FAMILY WALK
A visit to the office of the Burns Bog Conservation Society at 11961 - 88th Avenue, Delta (572-0373) is worthwhile. The society provides illustrated leaflets and conducts tours through the bog. Their office is open from 11:00 a.m. to 5:00 p.m. Tuesday to Saturday.

BURNS BOG. A GARBAGE DUMP? Future site of housing, golf courses, industrial development? Four thousand ha (10,000 acres) of waste land prone to fires? It doesn't sound too attractive. In fact, Burns Bog is a vast wilderness of unusual beauty where arctic plants such as cloudberry and reindeer moss survive among quaking mounds of sphagnum and miniature lodgepole pines. It is home to deer, foxes, coyotes, skunks, raccoons, rodents, frogs and a small number of black bears. A hundred and fifty species of birds, including the endangered sandhill crane, visit or nest in the bog; the rare mariposa copper butterfly has been found there. The whole is a priceless legacy from the ice age and the largest raised peat bog on the west coast of North America.

Why preserve it? As well as its value to wildlife, a wetland such as this aids in flood control and acts as a purification filter for the Fraser River's teeming salmon. Bog plants help to clean our atmosphere by converting carbon dioxide into plant matter. The hard-working Burns Bog Conservation Society, based in Delta, spearheads the ongoing battle to save the bog. At present, official public access to the bog is restricted to the Delta Nature Reserve, a fragment of bog forest in the northeast corner squeezed between highways and railroad—a mere 5 per cent of the total area, representative only of the bog's outer fringes.

Work is presently being done to repair the trails and boardwalks and to enlarge the walking possibilities within the reserve. One such new trail is included in the route described, and though a little rough in places at the time of writing, it can be followed without difficulty and allows walkers to venture into an interesting open area. The unusual approach via the Great Pacific Forum (don't hesitate to try their Boomer's Grill) is suggested by the B.B.C.S. as an improvement over the original trailhead at 108th Street and Monroe Drive, which necessitated a steep descent, some confusing paths and a crossing of the railway tracks. The reserve affords no expansive views—you have to look down and look closely to observe the bog's features and try to imagine the magical, watery, pristine acres beyond, where Tsawwassen women once came to gather berries.

If you head towards the corner of the Great Pacific Forum building you'll see a pink brick pathway. Follow this to the left, passing under the road, then switch to the gravel service road on the left and set off eastward along it. The first turning to the right, opposite a pylon, leads to a platform with benches and is the exit point of the new trail along which you can return. For now, continue on the service road for a further five minutes to the next turning to the right, a boardwalk that takes you in among bushes of hardhack and Labrador tea and lodgepole pines.

In this nutrient-poor habitat the pines may not have the stately bearing their name implies, but they are highly adaptable trees capable of surviving in some form in bogs and subalpine regions, on rocky headlands and coastal dunes. An intriguing feature of the bog proper is the diminishing size of these trees, from normal forest to twisted seventy-year-old specimens less than 2 metres (6 feet) tall. Under these conditions, they are often referred to as scrub or shore pines. The needles of lodgepole pines are stiff and twisted, attached in pairs. In spring, clusters of reddish pollen cones appear at the branch tips. The prickly brown seed cones can remain closed on the tree for years, able to withstand fire if necessary, and release their seeds later.

The boardwalk opens out to a platform from which you may contemplate the strange sight of a half-submerged piece of machinery. A few years ago, this bulldozer was stolen from a construction site and dri-

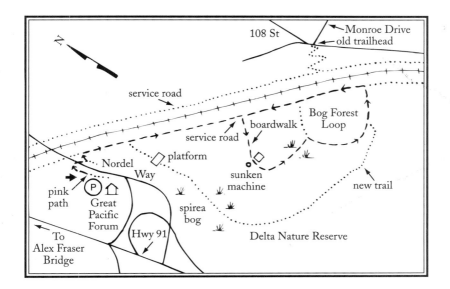

ven into the bog. Within a day it sank three metres into the peat and has since defied all efforts to extricate it. An unnatural sight, but it does illustrate the nature of a peat bog.

You can continue on the boardwalk over mounds of spongy sphagnum and patches of salal, until the ground becomes firmer and larger pines and cedars appear. However, a side trip into a clearing on the right, where there is a bench, will prove how unstable the ground is only a few metres from the trail. After a swampy section, redolent with skunk cabbage, you arrive at a junction with the Bog Forest Loop Trail. Turn right and proceed through a more established forest of hemlocks, cedars and Sitka spruce. In fall, many fungi can be found in this area—conical brown toadstools lacking only an elf, neat round patches of white mushrooms so tiny you need a hand lens to examine them, and occasional large brown boletus mushrooms resembling sticky buns.

Watch for a trail heading right: this is your point of decision. The Bog Forest Loop Trail swings left and emerges on the service road, along which you can return directly to the parking lot. The newer, right-hand trail takes a wider sweep through the reserve to end at the platform mentioned earlier, close to the beginning of your walk. There is little difference in the distance to be covered, but until such time as it is finished, the new trail may be rough underfoot in places.

Those who choose to return this way will pass first through a semi-open area, followed by a stretch of dark, bare forest. Soon, birch and

cascara saplings creep in, and a thicket of Pacific crabapple. This shrubby tree, with its thorny spurs and untidy branches, is apt to show up anywhere—along streams and estuaries, in fields and swamps, even above beaches. It is most noticeable in April and May when showy clusters of pinkish-white blossom perfume the air. It is our only native apple tree and is still valued by coastal aboriginal people for its tart little apples, which can be preserved in water and their own acidity.

Perhaps stepping over the cut stems of Labrador tea, you work your way out into the open. A sea of huckleberry, blueberry, spirea and sweet gale stretches on either side, but birdsong and the buzz of insects and the bog's own rustling, whispery sounds are overwhelmed by the incessant noise of the nearby highway and the constant drone of aircraft overhead—reminders of the vulnerability of this unique environment. After a belt of small pines you will come to the platform and final stretch of boardwalk to the service road.

HOW TO GET THERE: From Highway 91 south, take the first exit south of the Alex Fraser bridge, signed "Nordel Way/River Road." Keep right towards River Road and continue past the commercial weighing station and through the traffic lights, then turn right on Nordel Court. Drive to the end of the road and into the Great Pacific Forum parking lot. Park at the east side of the lot, close to the (overhead) Nordel Way. Journey time: 30 minutes.

FACING PAGE: *Lodgepole pine pollen cones*

21
Deas Island

HIGHLIGHTS
River, slough, tidal marsh, meadows, dunes; historic buildings; Scotch broom, horsetails, aquatic plants; eagles' nest, songbirds, diving birds, raptors; seals

SEASON
All year

ROUND TRIP
4.5 km (2 ½ miles)

TERRAIN
Flat. Dyke-top and woodland trails, sandy paths.

FAMILY WALK
There are riverside picnic tables as well as a group picnic shelter near the Fisher's Field parking lot. Heritage buildings include a Queen Anne-style residence, furnished with collectibles, and a one-room schoolhouse.

ALTHOUGH DEAS ISLAND IS NOW linked by a causeway to the mainland, it remains an island at heart. The main channel of the Fraser River sweeps along its western shore, while the sheltered water of the slough lies on the eastern side. True to its island nature, Deas is often windy, and nature walkers should dress accordingly.

The seasons transform this river environment. A winter walk offers a primordial scene—an apparently lifeless swamp, a ghostly sun shining through river fog, muddy or frozen trails. But among the skeletal bushes, towhees, juncos and chickadees will be scratching out their living. Come again in spring, when the island hums with bird and insect life, the leaves are yellow green and wildflowers fringe the marsh.

Some other attractions of this lively little regional park are picnic areas, a group campground and a boat dock. Three historic buildings have been brought to the park and restored for use.

Fog on Deas Island

Head west along the riverbank to begin your walk with an overview of the river from the observation tower. In spring you may see grebes and mergansers diving for eulachon; later in summer, thousands of migrating salmon, their presence marked by seals and gillnetters, fight the current on their journey upstream to spawning grounds in the watershed. Tugs, booms and fishing boats also go about their business, and the occasional freighter glides by. A plaque near the information stand tells of an enterprising tinsmith named John Sullivan Deas who claimed the island in 1873, building and operating a successful fish cannery upon it. So off you go along the Tinmaker's Walk.

This treed dyke cuts through a forest of cottonwood and alder—an unusually large old alder stands on the right of the track a short distance from the beginning—with an undergrowth of elderberry, snowberry and blackberry bushes. High in a cottonwood tree to the left of the trail is an eagles' nest of immense size. This may best be observed through binoculars from Fisher's Field later in the walk. As early as January you might see the resident eagles carrying new sticks to add to the already

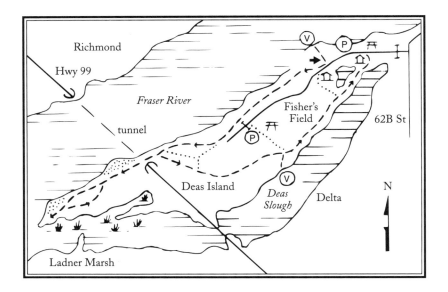

massive structure. Because of their size, eagles must build their nests clear of surrounding branches, so snags and bare treetops are chosen; it is not uncommon for the weight of an eagles' nest to bring down the snag upon which it is constructed. Only two eggs are laid in the lofty edifice, the eaglets flying after about seventy to seventy-five days.

Keep right onto Riverside Walk. The trees soon give way to a more open, sandy area where Scotch broom has moved in. Unlike its relative, gorse, of which it is said, "When the gorse is not in bloom, kissing's out of fashion," broom flowers circumspectly in May and June. By August, small hairy pods hang from the branches, ready to twist and open, catapulting the seeds for several feet. This distribution can be aided further by the wanderings of ants, who, attracted to the oily-coated seeds, carry them off along their highroads.

Island Tip Trail, which you have now joined, passes Sand Dune Trail on the left (your return route) and crosses Highway 99 where that arterial route disappears into the George Massey Tunnel beneath your feet. From then on the path proceeds informally to the western tip of the island, as far as a seat overlooking a tiny beach. Beyond this, you must pick your way over the debris left by winter's high tides to look across the mouth of Deas Slough towards Ladner Marsh.

After retracing your steps over the tunnel, take Sand Dune Trail on the right. First you pass through a boggy area of young conifers amid dense stands of scouring rush. This member of the horsetail family sends up a hollow, ribbed shoot, jointed like a fishing rod, which lasts for several years, so that even a winter walk can be brightened by the miniature grey-green forest. The plant spreads by creeping underground stems, as all gardeners know. A hard, sharply pointed cone is borne at the tip of the green stalk. All horsetails are impregnated with silica, giving them an abrasive quality once valued by native peoples for polishing wooden utensils and arrow shafts. As you tread the paths cut through the beds of this vigorous plant, you can ponder the fact that tree-sized horsetails existed in prehistoric times.

Keep right when you meet Dyke Loop Trail to reenter the woods on a wide track bordered by snowberry bushes. Having taken this walk on more than one Christmas morning, I can vouch for the decorative effect of the fluffy white snowberries clinging to the bare twigs. Unmarked side paths to the right are pleasant, though inconclusive, as they wander among the persistent horsetails. Don't pass up the signposted side trail, however, leading to a viewpoint overlooking Deas Slough. From the bench beside a woodpeckered tree you can watch the comings and goings of waterfowl and herons on their daily round.

Although Deas Slough is manmade, created by the construction of the connecting causeway, the rich aquatic habitat it provides is the same as that of any natural backwater formed over time by the gradual changing and silting up of a channel. Home to small fish such as shiners and sticklebacks, as well as to tiny shrimp, snails and insect larvae that could not survive in the river currents, the slow-moving water is also a temporary haven and feeding ground for juvenile salmon at the beginning of their ocean life. Aquatic plants, bacteria and plankton are essential links in the food chain that begins in the life-giving mud of the slough.

Continuing, you will find that Slough View Trail soon opens out into a meadow, named Fisher's Field, where your progress might be slowed by the river sand underfoot. From here you can train your binoculars on the eagles' nest and watch for other raptors hunting over the field. To complete the circuit, go right on Tidal Pool Trail. After emerging near the old Inverholme schoolhouse, walk west along the road or riverbank to your car.

HOW TO GET THERE: Travelling south on Highway 99, take the Victoria Ferry exit 28 and follow the River Road sign left across the overpass. Proceed north on 62B Street for about 2.5 km (1½ miles), following Deas Island Regional Park signs. Leave your car in the first parking lot on the right. Journey time: 20 minutes.

22
Boundary Bay

HIGHLIGHTS
Tidal lagoon, beach, dunes; dune plants, field flowers; gulls, shorebirds, ducks, raptors; cottontails, muskrats

SEASON
All year. Winter for ducks and raptors, spring and fall for migratory shorebirds.

ROUND TRIP
4 km (2 ½ miles)

TERRAIN
Flat. Dyke, foreshore and field path.

FAMILY WALK
Picnic tables and a beach are located at the south end of the park.

TUCKED INTO THE SOUTHWEST CORNER of the 16-km (10-mile)–wide Boundary Bay, this regional park provides opportunities to view large concentrations of wintering and migratory birds. Like the Fraser estuary, the tidal bay is an important stopover in spring and fall for geese and shorebirds on their way between their northern breeding grounds and the southern regions where they pass the winter. Migrating birds must pause during these arduous journeys to rebuild their energy by resting and feeding, and so we witness the arrival and departure of flocks of western sandpipers, dowitchers and yellowlegs as well as hundreds of Brant geese. Some shorebirds, such as sanderling and dunlin, go no farther, but winter in the bay along with thousands of ducks and diving birds. Resident hawks, owls and eagles are joined in winter by fellow raptors; swallows and warblers fly in for the summer to share the pickings of the fields inside the dyke.

Keen bird-watchers will want to visit Boundary Bay during the winter months when the lagoon teems with mallards, widgeon, northern

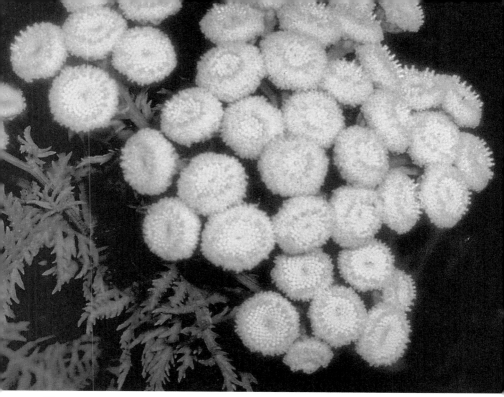

Tansy

pintail, green-winged teal, scaup, surf scoters and Barrow's goldeneyes, and grebes, loons and cormorants are diving in the open bay. Here, I have chosen to describe the walk in late summer, when lazy beachcombers and picnickers can explore the unique world of the dunes, enjoy the flowers along the dyke and watch the first of the sandpipers skimming over the water.

Go through the gate onto the dyke and you will find yourself looking upon a tidal lagoon. At low tide this may be an expanse of mud, grass and channels inhabited by groups of preening or sleeping ducks and an occasional killdeer calling its own name. If you see a small, handsome gull with a black head and bill feeding in the shallows, you have probably spotted a Bonaparte's gull, one of many gull species that frequent the bay. An observation platform has been erected on the dyke (thoughtfully provided with a ramp for wheelchairs) from which you can look out over the lagoon and its sheltering sandbar. At low tide, beds of glasswort are visible, a leafless salt-marsh plant sometimes called sea asparagus and deemed edible. Beyond the sandbar, flocks of gulls rest on the beach, all facing into the wind; farther out, herons are posted like sentinels in the shallow water. The mudflats and sandbars of the bay support extensive eelgrass meadows, an important food source for waterfowl, attracting in particular the large flocks of Brant geese in March and April.

In summer, the landward side of the dyke is a riot of tansy, golden-rod, thistles, yarrow and the yellow flowers of sticky, salt-loving gumweed. Swallows streak along the ditches between ranks of purple-spired loosestrife to the accompaniment of a grasshopper orchestra. Later, you can explore the abandoned farmland inside the dyke by following unofficial (though well-used) paths that bring you back to the bridge near the pumphouse.

As you turn southward along the dyke, the bay opens out before you. Here you may see sandpipers running and probing at the water's edge. On a winter walk, you'll see flocks of dunlin along the foreshore—look for a greyish shorebird with white underparts and a down-curved bill. And if you are lucky you may witness the dunlins' spectacular aerial tactics when threatened by a hungry falcon. Closing ranks, thousands of birds form a dense flock that swoops, soars and rolls with disciplined precision, now dark against the sky, now flashing white underparts in the sun—a confusing, high-speed mass of bodies that no bird of prey would risk penetrating.

The foreshore is composed of bands of grass, sand and pebbles. If you choose to pick your way over the driftwood below the dyke, you'll find clumps of silver burweed, an unusual member of the aster family with silvery, deeply divided leaves and spikes of greenish disk flowers. Searocket grows happily in the sand too, the tips of its sprawling branches bearing small, pale purple flowers. By late August the upper part of the beach will be dotted with the spiky brown seedheads of large-headed sedge, a heavily armoured beach plant that sends up its sharply pointed leaves and formidable fruit from long, straight rhizomes in the sand.

The land inside the dyke can be observed from a boardwalk that begins near the observation tower. After strolling between beds of cattails and bulrushes, past thickets of wild rose and blackberry bushes entwined with bittersweet, you come to open dunes where beach grasses and large-headed sedge predominate. A loop trail furnished with information panels tells the story of these pioneer plants that anchor the shifting sand with long rhizomes, gradually building a stable habitat for other plants.

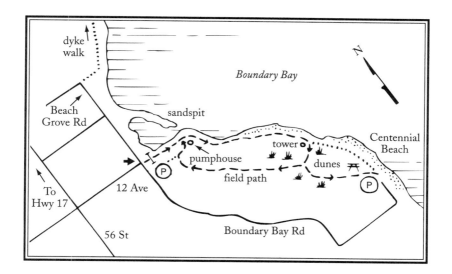

The dune paths lead eventually to the civilized corner of the park. A visit to Boundary Bay would not be complete without sitting on the beach for a while, enjoying whatever comes into your line of vision—Mount Baker towering above the eastern horizon; a determined swimmer wading patiently through the shallow water.

To return to 12th Avenue by the field paths, retrace your steps through the dunes towards the observation tower, until you spot a trail heading northward along the west side of a belt of alder and cottonwood. Perching or circling hawks can almost always be spotted here, and occasionally owls, for the untended fields, hedges and shallow sloughs provide a harvest of rabbits and small rodents for the hunters. Coyotes, too, take their share. Red-winged blackbirds and bands of savannah sparrows are a sign that you are approaching the deep ditch below the main dyke, where the wooden bridge near the pumphouse is the only crossing place. As you cover the final few metres to the parking lot, you will be able to see that, beyond the waterfront houses on Beach Grove Road, there are many more miles of walkable dyke around the bay to explore on future visits.

HOW TO GET THERE: From Highway 99 south take Highway 17 (Victoria Ferry) exit 28. Turn left (south) for Tsawwassen on 56th Street and left on 12th Avenue to its end at the junction with Boundary Bay Road. There is a small parking area at the entrance to the dyke. Journey time: 45 minutes.

23
Houston Trail

DERBY REACH REGIONAL PARK
LANGLEY

HIGHLIGHTS
Forest, farmland, riverbank; Fraser River, historic site, heritage buildings; broadleaf and vine maples; licorice fern, fungi; woodland birds; rabbits

SEASON
All year

ROUND TRIP
5.5 km (3 ½ miles)

TERRAIN
Some ups and downs. Well-groomed forest trails and gravel path.

FAMILY WALK
There is an inviting picnic area at the Houston heritage site, and extensive riverside picnic grounds at Edgewater Bar. It is only a ten-minute drive to Fort Langley's restored Hudson's Bay Company fort.

DERBY REACH REGIONAL PARK lies along the south shore of the Fraser River a few kilometres west of Fort Langley. One entrance is at Edgewater Bar on Allard Crescent, where the excellent salmon fishing lures thousands of anglers every year, many taking advantage of the overnight campsites provided. Between June and September millions of sockeye and chinook salmon make their way up the river, followed by coho in late summer and chum during October and November. Spawning runs of steelhead and cutthroat trout occur throughout the winter. Lately, disquieting records indicate that the Fraser's salmon runs, historically among the largest in the world, have become unpredictable. At Edgewater Bar there is ample parking for day visitors, and an easy 1 km- (½ mile-) trail through the woods and along the access road, beneath giant black cottonwood trees. Another entrance to the park is located about 2 km (1 mile) east of Edgewater Bar, on Allard Crescent, where a

Fort–to–Fort Trail

cairn marks the site of the original Fort Langley, then known as Derby Townsite. For a short, easy walk along a portion of the newly constructed Fort-to-Fort Trail, this is a good starting point. For the satisfying, circular route described here, including forest, meadow, riverbank and heritage site, start from the Houston Trailhead on McKinnon Crescent, as directed.

A clockwise circuit works well, so set off on the trail to the left of the information stand. The good gravel path winds gently up and down through a mixed forest where broadleaf maples predominate, with a shrub layer of vine maple, alder, hazelnut and elderberry bushes. Ferns and occasional patches of Oregon grape cover the ground, augmented in spring and summer by a trailside fringe of large-leaved avens and yellow violets.

It seems that the limbs and trunk of every tree in the woodland are clothed with moss; the broadleaf maples, especially, support several kinds of moss and fronds of licorice fern. This evergreen fern, also found in mats on mossy rock faces, loves the nonacid bark and high cal-

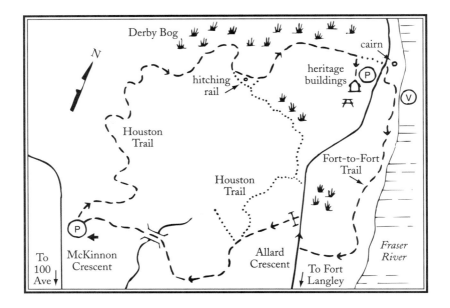

cium content of broadleaf maple. It spreads by thick, horizontal rhizomes from which individual fronds appear at intervals. The rhizomes, which have a licorice taste, were chewed by coastal Indians as a medicine for colds.

Farther along, after passing a damp depression on the left, you will come upon a huge broadleaf maple leaning beside the trail and quite covered with epiphyte (the name given to a plant that grows on another living plant) ferns and mosses. Of all Canada's maples, only the broadleaf, vine and Douglas maples are native to British Columbia. The broadleaf, as its name implies, has the largest leaf of any maple, up to 30 cm (12 inches) across and divided into five lobes. In April, as the leaves are unfurling, clusters of pale green flowers hang from the twigs. All maples have winged fruits, called samaras, to carry the seeds; those of the broadleaf maple are V-shaped and golden-brown. The bark is deeply furrowed.

In damp places, and at the edges of the forest where sunlight penetrates, multitrunked vine maples spread their arching branches. Their roundish leaves, with seven to nine shallow lobes, light up the woods in fall with brilliant reds and golds. The wings of the vine maple fruits are spread wide and turn reddish-brown when ripe. The Douglas maple, though sometimes found among its coastal relatives, prefers a drier site and is more common in the interior and parts of Vancouver Island. Its small, three- to five-lobed leaves of typical maple leaf shape are eye-catching in fall as they turn through yellow and orange to crimson. The hard but flexible wood of both Douglas and vine maples was used by aboriginal peoples to make masks and snowshoe and saddle frames, the green wood being soaked, then heated and moulded into shape.

More conifers vie with the deciduous trees along the northern edge of the forest, and you are likely to hear the voices of squirrels, wrens and Steller's jays as you follow the winding path. After a bend to the right, you enter a grove of tall, straight hemlocks with foamflower dancing airily at their feet. Finally, the light floods in as you emerge into a clearing where bracken, grass and blackberry bushes provide a habitat for rabbits. At the end of the clearing is a hitching rail for horses, and a parting of the ways. Yours is the left-hand trail.

Now you are on your way to the river. After crossing a bridge and passing a field on the right, you may notice some ponds to the left of the trail. This is the edge of Derby bog, a tract of peat bog and wetland destined to be preserved but without public access at present. When you come within sight of the road, turn off into the heritage site through the small gate on the right. At the time of writing the heritage buildings were not open to the public, but it is interesting to stroll through the site and view the barn and farmhouse from the outside.

The Houston homestead was built in 1890 and the Karr/Mercer barn, originally located in Rosedale, in 1872. There is also a whitewashed milkhouse and a small wooden structure in danger of falling backwards whilst waiting for restoration. Some splendid Douglas firs, cedars and spruce grace the site. Across the road an inscription on the cairn describes the spot as the first permanent British settlement in the lower Fraser Valley and the original site of the Hudson's Bay Company fort, relocated in 1858 to its present site in Fort Langley, a few kilometres upstream.

A path leads past an English oak to a wooden fence on the cliff top, from which you can view a long sweep of the Fraser River and a stretch of the north shore from Maple Ridge to Mission, with its monastery perched upon the hill. Steps lead down to a sand and gravel beach, usually occupied by stern-faced anglers, watching their lines from the comfort of camp chairs. Adjacent to the cairn is a sign announcing the Fort-to-Fort Trail, a proposed walking and cycling route from the original site of the fort to its present location. The completed section of the trail lying within Derby Reach Park can be used to link up with the Houston Trail and makes a pleasant variation from the forest circuit. You can, of course, retrace your steps to the hitching post and walk every foot of the Houston Trail if you prefer, in which case you will enjoy a lovely stretch of coniferous forest, add 1 km (½ mile) to your day's outing, and climb a surprisingly steep hill.

Let us suppose you have opted for the Fort-to-Fort Trail. A wide gravel path heads across a field towards the river, skirts some wild rose and blackberry patches and passes through a stand of alder to a viewing platform on the edge of the bluff. Idling away time here on a September afternoon, I have watched the Albion ferry plying between Fort Langley and Mission, tugboats ploughing upstream against the current, and the paddlewheeler from New Westminster Quay churning past with end-of-season sightseers. Two harbour seals surfaced to stare around, and then dived again, and I was visited briefly by a downy woodpecker, a serious little fellow dressed in black and white with a small red cap on the back of his head.

Staying away from the unstable cliff edges, the trail winds instead through rolling fields of meadow grass, clover and thistles, passing a duck pond and several old apple trees along the way. As it approaches private property, the path swings inland to end abruptly back at Allard Crescent, leaving subsequent stretches of the route to be explored at a later date, as they are completed. For now, turn right on the road and walk back for about 200 metres to a gated track entering the woods on the left. This, after a few minutes of walking, brings you to a junction with the Houston Trail, along which you turn left to complete your circular ramble.

In fall especially, you might spot some interesting fungi as you wander through these tangled woods. Multicoloured shelf fungus can be found on the trunks and stumps of deciduous trees year-round, ranging from rows of small, wavy-edged or bright yellow ears to thick brown and white brackets up to 30 cm (12 inches) across. A close look at decaying logs and branches might yield greenish-yellow sulphur tops or gruesome-sounding dead man's fingers. Ignore all side trails, and you will eventually descend to a bridge with a low log guardrail; five minutes later you are back at the Houston trailhead, where you began your country odyssey.

HOW TO GET THERE: Leave Highway 1 at the 200th Street exit 58 and drive north on 200th Street. Turn right (east) on 96th Avenue, left (north) on 216th Street, right on 100th Avenue, then left on McKinnon Crescent. The signposted Houston Trailhead is on the right, a short distance north of 102nd Avenue. Journey time: 1 hour.

24
Campbell River Loop

CAMPBELL VALLEY REGIONAL PARK
SOUTH LANGLEY

HIGHLIGHTS
Woodland, stream and meadow; wildflowers, sedges; herons, songbirds; Douglas squirrels

SEASON
All year, but prone to flooding in wet weather.

ROUND TRIP
2.3 km (1 ½ miles)

TERRAIN
Flat. Boardwalks and smooth trails, suitable for wheelchairs.

FAMILY WALK
From the 16th Avenue parking lot you can drive via 200th Street to the south entrance on 8th Avenue where the facilities include a visitor centre, wildlife garden and picnic tables. Nearby is the Annand/Rowlatt farmstead and a schoolhouse dating from 1924.

FROM THE MANY INTERESTING TRAILS in the park, I have chosen to describe a summer stroll beside the Little Campbell River, not only for its variety but also because its level terrain is suitable for wheelchairs and baby strollers. There is much to interest children—who is better at spotting frogs and tadpoles?—and the walk could be combined with a picnic at either of the park entrances. The early settlement of the valley is described in the leaflets provided at the information stand, which also distributes a map showing the entire hiking and equestrian trail system. Today's walk is shown on the park map as Little River Loop Trail.

Set off on the path heading east from the information stand. Beneath the maples and Douglas firs are beds of false lily-of-the-valley and star-flowered Solomon's-seal, by July their modest flowers already being replaced by berries. Hazelnut shrubs, common in the valley, will now be sporting clusters of pale green, husk-covered nuts. This spot is also delightful in spring, when the first trilliums brighten the awakening woods.

As you step out of the trees onto a boardwalk, you may be surprised to find that the grandly named Little Campbell River is a sluggish brown stream amid a vast water meadow. This is its summer habit; in winter it may slide beneath a sheet of ice or flood the valley bottom, drowning the walkways. Crossing the marsh in summer, you are surrounded by wild roses, hardhack and ninebark shrubs; branching stalks of water parsley vie with skunk cabbage and sedges; yellow water lilies find a toehold and cattails poke their heads from the sea of greenery. Don't be startled if a great blue heron suddenly takes to the air, croaking its annoyance at being disturbed—a sound that briefly silences the foraging songbirds. As the hunter settles again beside a reedy channel, birdsong resumes.

Noticeable from the boardwalk are stands of small-flowered bulrush. This sturdy plant grows from a thick rhizome, producing broad, grasslike leaves and clusters of nodding flower spikes on spreading stalks. A useful guideline, "Sedges have edges and rushes are round," helps to identify this plant as a sedge, the stem being slightly triangular. Beyond this, it would take special study to understand the complexities of grasses, sedges and rushes. All of them can provide valuable forage and habitat for wildlife. Many, like tules and small-flowered bulrush, were woven by aboriginal peoples into mats and baskets.

At the eastern edge of the marsh, you might spot the blue saucer-shaped flowers of American brooklime. Like the marsh forget-me-nots that thrive around Beaver Lake in Stanley Park, this plant grows happily with its feet in shallow water. As you turn and head southward beneath the trees, woodland flowers such as herb Robert and enchanter's nightshade appear. Scarlet baneberries catch the eye, the shiny clusters thrusting above the crinkly, three-lobed leaves. Every part of this striking member of the buttercup family is highly poisonous.

You are almost sure to see Douglas squirrels along this stretch of trail. This small, olive-brown squirrel with a buffy-orange belly, sometimes called the chickaree, is native to the west coast, unlike its larger grey and black cousins which come from eastern Canada. The chickaree almost flies among the branches as it collects its diet of seeds and nuts. Cone seeds are its favourite, and caches of cones are diligently made, but fruit and fungi are acceptable too, as is the birdseed scattered on the trail by visitors. On a fine Sunday afternoon, I have spotted replete squirrels dozing in the crooks of branches above the heads of passing

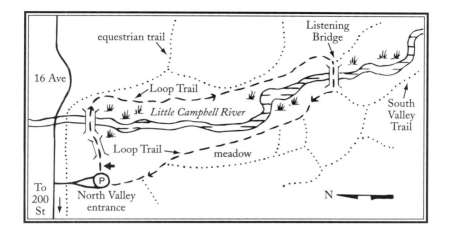

nature lovers. More often, though, the nimble rodents are going about their business, an important aspect of which is to treat intruders to a tongue lashing, shattering the peace of the forest with a burst of rapid, scolding notes.

The trail passes beneath some fine western red cedars and large broadleaf maples before heading off to the right to recross the marsh and the meandering stream. A long boardwalk, known as the Listening Bridge, leads to a platform with benches—a wonderful place to sit for a while and take in the humming, twittering, buzzing and plopping sounds of the marsh in summer. Swallows and flycatchers feed on the wing; warblers and song sparrows dart among the shrubs, where long tendrils of bittersweet twine their heart-shaped leaves and violet flowers around the pink spires of hardhack. A rufous hummingbird appears from nowhere to sip from a purple hedge nettle flower and disappears on the instant. If you are accompanied by children, they will certainly have spotted several frogs by now, or a salamander. The interpretive panels are popular with the young set, and you might find it difficult to tear them away from this fascinating spot when you are ready to move on.

Leaving the boardwalk, you soon arrive at a trail junction, the left-hand path leading to the uplands of the south valley and entrance, the right-hand returning you to the 16th Avenue parking lot. After a short stretch in the shade of the forest, the scene changes yet again as you step out into an open meadow where, in summer, oxeye daisies cast a white haze over the waving grass. Lupins, fading by midsummer, have shared the limelight, while drifts of fireweed are beginning to blaze. Looking

closer, you will see a host of smaller field flowers, such as red clover, common St. John's wort and selfheal. Bushes of oceanspray take advantage of the open site, their arching stems laden with creamy white flowers, perhaps already beginning to fade into the brown, dry clusters that remain on the bushes all winter.

Often the ring-necked pheasant's crowing voice can be heard in the meadow, but in summer its brilliant feathers and scarlet wattle may be hidden by the tall grass. The black-headed grosbeak is less shy, and you could easily spot the black and cinnamon body and white-patched wings of the male as it hunts around the meadow for seeds and insects. Several species of owls nest in the park, and although the daytime visitor is unlikely to spot more than the fur or feathers of victims or an owl's regurgitated pellets, special owling nights are organized when the raptors are tempted to respond to tape recordings—but that's another outing.

The final part of your walk is through a forest of conifers and maples, the domain of cedar waxwings, wrens and chickadees, and quite soon you are back at your starting point, loop completed—but much of Campbell Valley left to explore.

HOW TO GET THERE: Leave Highway 1 at the Langley City 200th Street exit 58 and travel south for 14.5 km (9 miles) to 16th Avenue. Turn left (east) on 16th and follow signs to Campbell Valley Park North entrance. Or, 16th Avenue can be reached from the King George Highway 99A near White Rock, from where you proceed eastward to the intersection with 200th Street and follow signs as above. Journey time: 1 hour.

FACING PAGE: *Meadow with oxeye daisies*

25
Pepin Brook Trail

ALDERGROVE LAKE REGIONAL PARK
LANGLEY/ABBOTSFORD

HIGHLIGHTS
Forest, meadow and stream; wildflowers; Salish suckers

SEASON
All year

ROUND TRIP
4 km (2 ½ miles)

TERRAIN
Ups and downs. Forest and meadow trails.

FAMILY WALK
There is a sandy beach with picnic tables around the lake. A large picnic shelter in the adjoining field can be reserved for groups.

LET'S FIRST OF ALL CLEAR UP a misnomer: Aldergrove "lake" is in fact a spring-fed, manmade swimming pool, especially suitable for children. This makes the park a great place for a family picnic, as well as a nature walk. Cyclists and horse riders are also catered to in this 250-ha (625-acre) stretch of rolling countryside in the central Fraser Valley, but the Pepin Brook Trail has been designated for walkers only and offers a quiet ramble through woodland and riparian (streambank) meadow.

Although the trail is accessible and interesting at any time of year, I have described it here as a late spring walk, because that is my favourite time to go, when the wildflowers along the way are as welcome as old friends turning up after a long absence. Don't look for anything exotic— these are modest meadow and woodland sprites—but if it pleases you to know the names of things, take along a pocket wildflower guide.

Pepin Brook Trail begins a few metres left of the entrance to the parking lot. Beneath an arch of vine maple boughs you enter a lush forest of birch and alder, cedar, hemlock and moss-clothed broadleaf maples. Beds of bleeding heart and false lily-of-the-valley carpet the

Buttercups

ground in the company of sword fern and wood fern. The arched stems and broad, veined leaves of false Solomon's-seal are easy to spot, with their plumes of creamy, perfumed flowers. Sturdy clumps of large-leaved avens are noticeable, too, yellow buttercup-like flowers adorning the tips of the plants above the ragged three-lobed leaves. Later, a round brown burr will develop from the flower, with tiny hooks designed to catch on fur and clothing for the purpose of dispersal.

Two members of the saxifrage family hold their own in this company. The tall flower stalks of fringecup wave above the sea of greenery, each strung with small flowers ranging from greenish-white to red. You will have to look closely to see how the frilly petals form a fringe around the centre of the flower. Its cousin, foamflower, is even daintier, with a constellation of tiny white flowers dancing around thin, almost invisible stalks. In common with many saxifrages, these two plants grow from a compact mass of basal leaves. Saxifrages are a widespread family whose members can be found in forests, along streambanks and clinging to rocky outcrops.

As you walk along, the sharp tang of stinging nettles pervades the air from time to time, and you will no doubt notice that colonies of this unpopular plant have established themselves in the woodland's more open spaces. In May and June, the plants will be decorated with drooping clusters of greenish flowers. The sawtoothed nettle leaves are covered with hollow hairs, tiny weapons that secrete formic acid when touched and cause that tingling rash. A sweet revenge might be to cook up the leaves as greens, said to be tastier than spinach. Certain caterpillars feed upon the leaves with impunity, nettles being de rigeur in the development of the red admiral butterfly.

After passing the junction with Rock'n Horse Trail, you begin to descend towards Pepin Brook, glimpsed below amid a sea of greenery. Pacific crabapple overhangs the trail, its clusters of oval berries looking a little like green olives in early summer. The banks beneath are clothed with beds of herb Robert, a dainty member of the geranium family whose small pink flowers are borne on hairy stalks above feathery, deeply divided leaves. You might spot the triple, fan-shaped vanilla leaf along here, too, its spike of white flowers atop a thin stem poking from the centre of the leaf. When dried, the leaves have a faint vanilla scent, and they were used by the Salish people as a fly repellent. In winter, after the plant has died, you will often see skeleton vanilla leaves, a mere network of veins like fine lace spread on the forest floor.

A left turn at the bottom of the slope leads by way of a boardwalk to the bridge over Pepin Brook. On a warm spring day you will want to lean on the rail for a while, looking and listening. Wrens and towhees are busy foraging in and under the massed shrubs overhanging the stream—a tangle of hardhack, black twinberry and red osier dogwood. Overhead, swallows wheel and dart after the season's first mosquitoes. The scent of skunk cabbage hangs heavy in the air; sedges and grasses bend and wave with the water. Sticklebacks, minnows, dace, trout and

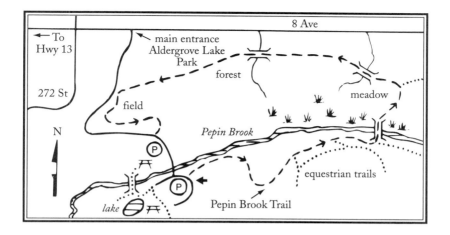

juvenile salmon frequent the streams of the Fraser Valley, and a notice beside the bridge will tell you that Pepin Brook is home also to an endangered species, the Salish sucker.

Suckers are bottom-feeding fish with a round, toothless mouth on the underside of the head, equipped with papillae (sensory projections) for detecting their chosen food of freshwater insect larvae. You may wonder, as I did, what is so special about Salish suckers. It is believed that eons ago, when ice covered the Fraser Valley and Puget Sound, certain longnose suckers became isolated from the rest of their clan by inhabiting a nonglaciated area between the ice sheet and the Columbia River. As the ice melted, these fish were able to move northward into the Fraser Valley. Since their range has remained separated from that of the longnose suckers to the present day, the characteristics gradually evolved by the isolated fish to suit their different environment have also persisted—hence a different sucker.

The distribution of the Salish sucker is confined to the Fraser Valley and a small area in northwest Washington, and some of these habitats are under siege. Pollution from sewage and pesticides, the removal of streamside vegetation where fish can hide and the diversion of watercourses all take their toll. Studies have shown that the Salish sucker is fast disappearing from our local streams. Only Pepin Brook supports a healthy population, perhaps because part of its course flows through parkland. If you are scanning the water for a sight of this ice-age survivor, look for an olive-coloured fish about the length of a hand. True to type, the sucker has a fairly long snout, rounded at the end, and a slightly forked tail.

When you are ready to move on, a gravel path leads away from the stream through meadows dotted with willows and yellow with buttercups in spring. Among the trailside plants are thistles and cow parsley, vetches and hawkweeds, all lovers of open spaces, along with a variety of graceful meadow grasses that no doubt hide the secret runways of voles and field mice.

After crossing a tributary stream below a waterfall, you climb to enter a forest of cedars and Douglas firs, where many large stumps bear witness to the original clearing of the land. Beds of vanilla leaf and enchanter's nightshade share the herb layer with ferns. These are peaceful woods, and the seat beside a bridge is well placed for rest and contemplation.

The scene changes once again as you emerge abruptly from the trees onto the bottom of a sloping field where hawthorn trees, perhaps planted when the land was settled, have taken hold. In spring, clouds of white blossom adorn the trees, the heady scent vying with the pervading sweetness of Scotch broom, which also grows in profusion on the slope. As you approach the park access road opposite the information stand, you will see that your path heads left up the grassy hill. The building at the top houses a telescope used by the Royal Astronomical Society on their viewing nights.

From the top of the field you descend once more beneath Douglas firs and huge old broadleaf maples to Sedge Field, opposite the group picnic shelter. If you wish to end your walk with a visit to the lake, a path leads from the far end of the shelter, across one last bridge over Pepin Brook, to the beach.

HOW TO GET THERE: Leaving Highway 1 at exit 73, drive south on Highway 13 (264th Street) to a left turn onto 8th Avenue. Soon after crossing 272nd Street, turn right at the Aldergrove Lake Park sign and proceed to the final parking area, near the lake. Journey time: 1 hour.

26
Cedars Mill Trail

LYNN HEADWATERS REGIONAL PARK
NORTH VANCOUVER

HIGHLIGHTS
River and forest; mountain views, mill site relics; devil's club, wildflowers; ravens

SEASON
May to November

ROUND TRIP
Up to 7.5 km (4 ½ miles)

TERRAIN
Mostly flat. Forest trail with one stony section and a few steps.

FAMILY WALK
Children will be sure to spot the bits of rusted machinery scattered around the old mill site—perhaps even an old boot or a battered cooking pot.

THE UPPER LYNN CREEK VALLEY, once watershed, was opened to the public in 1985. Today, hiking trails and back country routes enable the experienced hiker to explore the slopes and peaks of this rugged mountain region. From a level trail along the valley bottom, the less ambitious walker can share the wilderness experience with far less effort. Always within sound of fast-flowing Lynn Creek, the Cedars Mill Trail offers forest, beach and mountain views as well as reminders of former mining and logging days. Choose your season carefully— snow and ice can linger in Lynn Valley and even this low-elevation trail can be treacherous, especially in thawing conditions and periods of heavy rainfall. Also, the park provides extensive habitat for black bears, and although these animals are rarely encountered by the casual walker, to talk or whistle as you go along will lessen the chance of an unlooked-for meeting. If you do come across a bear, park authorities advise staying calm and slowly backing away until it is safe to proceed.

To get on your way, head past the information stand opposite the historic Mills House and cross Lynn Creek on the footbridge. Sign in at the hiker registration board (this information is for search and rescue purposes), and put away your own copy of the registration, which you must deposit in the box on your return. Now set off through the gate on the left, along the Lynn Loop Trail. From the wide gravel track beneath the evergreens you can glimpse the creek running swiftly over smooth rocks in its impetuous dash to the canyons downstream. Before long your route becomes rock-strewn, bearing witness to past flooding. Up ahead, you'll see that much work has been done to deter the turbulent Lynn from taking this wayward course.

In a short distance you reach a parting of the ways. Where Lynn Loop Trail heads off to the right in a series of switchbacks, you continue upstream on Cedars Mill Trail. After picking your way over a stony patch, you come to a boardwalk circumnavigating two huge root disks and the boggy hollow produced by their upheaval. Watch out next for a side path cutting through bracken to a viewpoint above the river. The cliff is giving way at the edge, so take care as you enjoy the view upstream and across the creek to Mount Fromme opposite.

After this rest, there are a few steps to climb and then more board-walks to take you through a marshy area and across a small ravine where the banks and trailside stumps are richly clothed with plants and mosses. You might spot the crooked stems and red, oval berries of twistedstalk in this plant paradise. Two bridges must be crossed, the second an old one with handrails at the site of the Cedars Mill, an operation that closed in 1927 but left a few mementoes for us to wonder at—a casual museum of rusted artifacts that lie, or hang, beside the trail.

In the vicinity of the 3.0 km marker, red ribbons mark a minor path heading left into the bushes. Although this diversion is not intended to be part of today's walk, it is worth mentioning for its destination. The rough route emerges eventually beside Lynn Creek, which adventurous hikers can ford (at low water only) to pick up a trail on the west bank leading to one of the largest remaining western red cedars in the Lower Mainland. This giant, measuring 4 metres (13 feet) in diameter and 55 metres (180 feet) in height, is believed to be more than six hundred years old.

Continuing upstream on the Cedars Mill Trail, you will shortly come to a fallen hemlock lying across the creek. The upturned root system has peeled away a layer of soil and vegetation to expose the ancient nurse log beneath. Walking on, past a belt of birches and willows on the

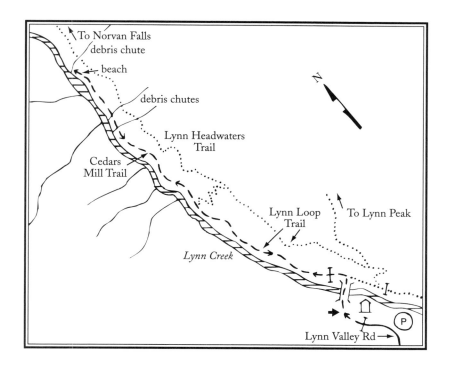

To Norvan Falls
debris chute
beach
debris chutes
Lynn Headwaters Trail
Cedars Mill Trail
Lynn Loop Trail
To Lynn Peak
Lynn Creek
Lynn Valley Rd →
N
P

creek side of the trail, you enter a grove carpeted with false lily-of-the-valley and patches of delicate, bright green oak fern. Throughout this wilderness walk you may have noticed the large maplelike leaves and crooked, spiny branches of devil's club along the trail. In June, clusters of small white flowers adorn the plant, later turning to eye-catching pyramids of bright red berries. The plant is related to ginseng and is still an important medicine for aboriginal peoples. Tea is made from the inner bark, and the stems are infused and drunk in the treatment of arthritis, ulcers and diabetes. The Squamish people used it in hot baths for rheumatism; others rubbed the berries into their scalps to discourage lice. The Haida Indians used the stems to hook octopus and to make fishing lures. Devil's club is abundant on the coast mountains and, in spite of its wicked armament, it often looks beautiful in the woods when its outspread leaves catch the sunlight.

Good views open out as you cross a debris chute on a wooden bridge. These seasonal channels, dry in summer, can become raging torrents during the spring runoff, hurling trees and boulders down the valley's steep sides. Soon after you leave the bridge, an opening on the river bank invites you to sit and enjoy the view of mountains and river, and

Bracket fungus

some might be content to make this their turnaround point. However, a further ten minutes of walking, through young alder and hemlocks, will bring you to the trail's end at the mouth of a large debris chute, where you can sit in an open area of shrubs, rocks and logs above the creek.

Perhaps, as you gaze upon the wide view of the valley and its surrounding peaks, you will yourself be watched by a soaring raven. The hoarse croak, ragged throat feathers and wedge-shaped tail in flight are the raven's familiar distinguishing features, but you may be surprised sometime to observe the tender family life of these fierce-looking birds. They may sit with heads together and converse in bell-like tones. Kisses may be exchanged, or courtship aerobatics performed, with upside-down flying and long tumbling falls in which the male and his lifelong mate are locked together. Nests are built in the tops of conifers.

When it is time to leave, retrace your steps by the same route, remembering, when you arrive back at your starting point, to sign out.

HOW TO GET THERE: From Highway 1 in North Vancouver, take Lynn Valley Road north, exit 19, and follow it for 4 km (2 ½ miles) to its end at Lynn Headwaters Regional Park. Journey time: 35 minutes.

27
Giant Fir Trail

HIGHLIGHTS
Forest and canyon; Cleveland dam, fish hatchery; giant Douglas firs, Pacific yews, nurse logs; wildflowers; woodpeckers

SEASON
All year

ROUND TRIP
1.2 km (¾ mile)

TERRAIN
Mostly flat, one short climb. Forest trails and service road.

FAMILY WALK
There is a covered picnic area near the hatchery. A bonus on this walk might be the spectacle of kayakers or canoeists practising or competing through the rapids below the weir.

THIS RUGGED 160-HA (400-ACRE) PARK extends for several miles along the Capilano River canyon. The area was logged around the turn of the century, but the second-growth forest is well established, with a handful of old-growth trees still standing. At the northern end of the park, the Cleveland dam, built in 1954 to provide water for Greater Vancouver, controls the flow of the river. The upper spawning beds having been flooded by the dam, fish swimming upstream are now diverted by a weir to the hatchery, and from May to December can be seen through a glass wall as they make their way up the fish ladder. Chinook and coho salmon and steelhead trout are reared at the hatchery, where displays explain their life cycle.

You will see from a park leaflet, available near the hatchery, that there are 26 km (16 miles) of trails to explore in addition to the short walk described here. The park is accessible all year, but keep in mind these are wilderness trails that can be hazardous when wet or snow-covered.

Your route, leading to the Giant Fir Trail, begins from the picnic area near the hatchery. Although I have described the walk in summer, its highlights are perennial. Find the trail that heads southward from the bus loop. The gnarled Pacific yew trees at its beginning (to identify, look for the flattened, sharply pointed needles with pale green undersides) are around two centuries old. Inside the scaly, weatherbeaten bark, yew wood is strong and durable. Native peoples of the Pacific Coast used it for making bows, harpoon shafts and canoe paddles as well as utensils and tools. The fruit of this coneless conifer is a single seed hidden inside each fleshy green berry, waiting until it is time to tempt the birds with the rosiness of September.

Cross the river on the wooden suspension bridge. In summer the water may be more green than white, more sliding than rushing, between the granite walls of the canyon. On the west bank, turn right and head back upstream.

Alongside the trail, the forest is busy with its eternal cycle of regeneration. Young hemlocks and huckleberry bushes reach up lustily from their nurse logs, while over the ground and the stumps and the roots grows a midsummer tangle of salmonberry, ferns and salal, laced with bunchberry and foamflower. A little farther on you enter a grove of tall, young conifers whose canopy has captured the sunlight, leaving a forest floor that is cool and dim with only an occasional clump of ferns drawing life from the bare ground.

You arrive at a fork in the trail. The left-hand path leads to the giant fir, but first, take time to walk along to Second Canyon for a view of the spillway of the Cleveland dam. During a rainy spell or spring runoff the platforms might be drenched with spray as water thunders through the canyon, but in summer only enough water may be released to help the fish swim from the ocean to their hatchery spawning beds.

Returning to the Giant Fir Trail, you must now climb five minor switchbacks to the benchland above the river. At the top, two old-growth Douglas firs stand to the left of the path. As well as surviving the early logging operations, these stalwarts bear scars of a forest fire. To the sun-loving Douglas fir, fire can be more friend than enemy. Occasional fires provide clearings where the Douglas fir seeds can germinate, and the young trees thrive unshaded in their race against the more shade-tolerant western hemlocks and cedars.

A little way ahead a sign directs you along a side trail to where the giant stands brooding over another opening in the forest. With a girth of 2.4 metres (8 feet) and a height of 60 metres (200 feet) to its broken

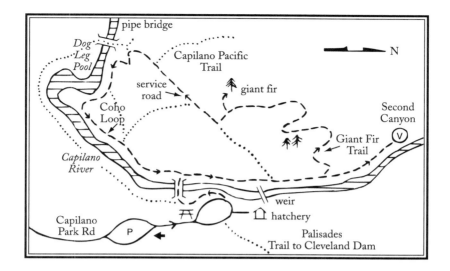

top, this is the largest of Capilano Canyon's old-growth Douglas firs. The tree is leaning slightly, and you'll see that several plants are growing from its upper side where rainwater has softened the bark. The bark on the lower side remains thick and corky with characteristic deep furrows, itself a protection to the mature tree from major fires. The reddish-brown cones of the Douglas fir can usually be found lying all around the trees, easily identifiable by their unique three-pointed bracts extending from the scales. Opposite the giant, an old log of immense length lies parallel to the trail, a host of plants and young trees growing on its back.

To make this a circular walk, return to the signpost and continue along the main trail. Turn right when you come to the service road. In summer your way is brightened by modest roadside flowers such as large-leaved avens and selfheal, plants that enjoy the extra sunlight the roadway provides. Selfheal, with its spires of hooded, purple flowers, is a member of the mint family and is purported to be a remedy for sore throat and other ills.

As you approach the river, a path to the left leads down to the pipeline bridge, from which you might spend a few minutes watching the river sweep out from the great loop of Dog Leg Canyon. For a level and easy route back to the hatchery, stay on the west bank, following the well-marked Coho Loop Trail.

The stumps and fallen logs of a coniferous forest provide food and shelter for a variety of creatures. Beetles, termites and carpenter ants live in and eat the decaying wood, and spiders and shrews feed on the

inhabitants of the fallen logs. More likely to be spotted by the walker in the forest is another dependent on rotting wood, the pileated wood-pecker. When you hear an imperative "cuk cuk cuk," watch for the flash of a brilliant red crest as this large woodpecker swoops between the trees to alight on a snag or stump. Gripping with strong, four-toed feet, tail pressed against the tree, it sets about the job of hammering for its diet of ants and wood-boring insects. For this heady work the wood-pecker is equipped with a specially designed, reinforced skull and an extensile tongue with which to probe for the grubs. The neat, rectangu-lar holes you may have seen in the trunks of dead, and sometimes living, trees, are its handiwork. For nesting, the pileated woodpecker chips out a large cavity, usually high in the tree, a residence that may later be taken over by squirrels, raccoons or owls. In nature, nothing is wasted.

You will soon find yourself back at the wooden suspension bridge near the picnic area. You might finish your outing with a visit to the fish hatchery or a trip to the Cleveland dam for a view of the Lions and the impounded Capilano Lake.

HOW TO GET THERE: From Highway 1 take the Capilano/Grouse Mountain exit 14 and drive north on Capilano Road to the fish hatch-ery turn-off (Capilano Park Road), a short distance beyond the traffic lights at Edgemont Boulevard. Journey time: 20 minutes.

By bus, you can take the No. 236 from Lonsdale Quay to the Capi-lano Park Road stop, but note that from there you will have a 1.5-km (1-mile) walk to the trailhead.

FACING PAGE: *Giant fir*

28
Goldie & Flower Lakes

MOUNT SEYMOUR PROVINCIAL PARK
NORTH VANCOUVER

HIGHLIGHTS
Subalpine lakes and meadows; mountain hemlock, yellow cedars; water lilies, queen's cup; chestnut-backed chickadees, blue grouse; salamanders; dragonflies

SEASON
July to October

ROUND TRIP
3.5 km (2 miles)

TERRAIN
Ups and downs. Forest trails, rough in places.

FAMILY WALK
End with a picnic overlooking the lake near the Mystery Peak chairlift.

MOUNT SEYMOUR PROVINCIAL PARK is a wilderness area encompassing both Western Hemlock and Mountain Hemlock zones. Goldie and Flower Lakes lie in the transitional subalpine region of the mountain, conveniently close to the upper parking lot. The trails are well maintained, given the rugged nature of the terrain, and walkers who can cope with some rocks and roots will be rewarded by this short excursion into the mountain wilderness. You can, of course, content yourself with a visit to Goldie Lake only—a round trip of 2 km (1½ miles); just follow the signs. But Flower Lake is different in character and it is a pity to miss it.

The park is home to coyotes, bears, cougars and deer, as well as small mammals such as squirrels, pine martens, voles and mice. Though most of these animals are rarely encountered, their tracks and signs are there to be read by an observant walker. A spongy, muddy trail can be an exciting record of the comings and goings of a region's inhabitants.

FACING PAGE: *Hemlock with U bend*

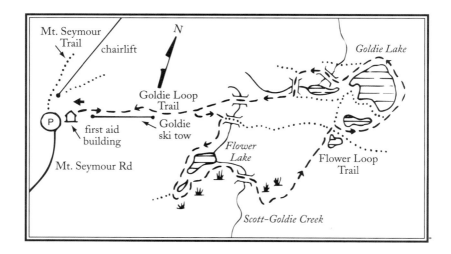

Boots are an advantage for this walk, also some protective clothing. Choose your day carefully—mountain weather can change very quickly, and even the most avid nature walker might not enjoy wandering in a maze of hiking trails amid cold, swirling cloud.

The Goldie and Flower Lakes Trail begins from the east side of the parking lot, behind the first-aid building. Start by descending on the track beside the Goldie ski tow. Raw though they are, ski slopes, with their sparse vegetation, do provide pickings for birds such as the blue grouse, and in summer or fall you could spot a hen with chicks feeding at the edge of the clearing. If you can visit as early as June, you'll hear the male grouse hooting from the trees.

At the bottom of the hill, watch for the hiking trail branching off to the right, into the woods. Twisted old mountain hemlocks lean over the path, with huckleberry, copperbush, blueberry and heather crowding in, all acid-tolerant plants capable of drawing nutrients from soil leached out by prolonged snowfall. Mats of mosslike mountain spirea, or partridgefoot, fringe the path, adorned with dense clusters of tiny white flowers in July and August.

Opposite a stand of Sitka mountain ash, take the signposted Flower Lake Loop Trail to the right. In a short distance you will come to some wet meadow patches and a stream, where again you turn right to Flower Lake. With the stream now gurgling on your left, you descend the rough path beneath majestic yellow cedars until Flower Lake comes into view, secluded and inviting on a sunny day, and quite covered with water lilies.

The end of the lake is marshy with meadow patches of false helle-bore and twistedstalk between small sedge-fringed ponds and channels. Boardwalks help you over the wettest places. As you begin to work your way along the wooded eastern side of the lake, look out for queen's cup, perhaps growing from a bed of conifer needles in company with bunch-berry. This beautiful forest lily has clumps of long, shiny leaves from which solitary, six-petalled white flowers shine like stars. Even more fascinating are the single bright blue berries that appear in September, their metallic sheen eye-catching among autumn's greens and golds. The plant is also known as beadlily.

At the northeast end of the lake, your trail heads off to the right. A log bridge spans the outlet creek, Scott-Goldie, followed by a curved boardwalk over a marsh. The trail then climbs through forest, eventu-ally passing a small lake on the right, to arrive at a major trail junction. To continue your anticlockwise circuit, go straight ahead between the two rocks and then immediately turn right, keeping another pond on your left.

After you cross a creek, Goldie Lake lies before you, a still, clear body of water painted with perfect reflections of the surrounding forest. A side trail left leads to a stretch of shoreline with rocks on which to sit and observe what is going on around you. And life is rich in ponds and shallow lakes.

Beyond the willows, sedges and rushes at the water's edge, floating and underwater plants grow, providing in their turn food and shelter for creatures such as leeches, snails, mosquito larvae, water beetles and fish. The flashing, iridescent dragonfly that darts briefly into your vision, giving rise to the usual feeling of wonder, is in fact a rapacious predator of pond and marsh. With large, many-faceted eyes, the dragonfly can spot its prey up to 40 metres (131 feet) away; unique aerodynamics allow forward, backward and sideways flight up to 100 km (60 miles) an hour. The insect meal is captured and devoured in flight.

Hatched from eggs laid under the leaves of aquatic plants, dragonfly nymphs are no less voracious. For two years or more they consume quan-tities of worms and crustaceans from the depths—unless, of course, they become a meal for a hungry fish themselves. Because the dragonfly's wingspan is fixed, the creatures can sometimes be seen resting briefly on a twig, wings outstretched. Fossils indicate that in prehistoric times dragonflies might have had a wingspan of two feet. Dragons indeed.

Peering down into the water you might spot another local denizen, the northwestern salamander. Prominent paratoid glands behind the eyes and a ridge along the top of the tail help to identify this chocolate-brown salamander. It is usually about 15 cm (6 inches) long and may be sporting feathery gills and tail fins, depending on its stage of development. The secretive amphibian leads a double life, spending part of its time on land beneath damp leaves or rotting logs, where it feeds on slugs and other soft invertebrates, migrating to the water in early spring to breed. An egg mass is attached to a submerged stick, the young hatching in about a month. Normally, the larvae take two or three years to reach maturity, but some larvae of the northwestern salamander never fully metamorphose, appearing to live full and happy lives in the water, even breeding in due season with properly transformed individuals.

When it is time to resume your circuit around the lake, you will come upon a place where huge rocks overhang the trail. One or two hemlocks have got a foothold in this unlikely spot, tough specimens that have developed U bends in their trunks to compensate for the difficult location and withstand the pressure of snow. In the mountains the struggle for survival goes on all the time, and plants and animals find unique ways to adapt to the harsh conditions.

Tree roots crisscross the trail as you round the northern end of the lake. Here, the banks on either side are covered with creeping raspberry, a tiny plant frequently present in mature forest though rarely noticed. Five-lobed leaves, delicate white flowers and, in September, clear red berries spring from a thin vine that trails along the forest floor and over stumps and logs.

Upon reaching the marshy end of the lake, follow the main trail as it crosses two creeks and heads in a westerly direction. On one occasion as I walked up through these woods, I noticed a scattering of tiny grey and yellow feathers on a log—the untimely end of a kinglet or warbler, perhaps the victim of another of the region's residents, the northern pygmy owl. A fierce little hunter, no larger than a starling, this owl is active in the daytime and might be spotted in a tree at the edge of a clearing, or its hollow-sounding "ook" might warn of its presence. Old woodpecker holes serve well as a nesting place for this owl.

Several small creeks are crossed before you find yourself back at the junction with the Flower Lake Loop Trail, circuit completed except for the last short climb back to your car in parking lot 4.

HOW TO GET THERE: From the Parkgate shopping centre on Mount Seymour Parkway in North Vancouver, drive north on Mount Seymour Road to its end at parking lot 4. Journey time: 40 minutes.

29
Seymour Valley

HIGHLIGHTS
Forest and lake; woodland birds, waterfowl; deer, squirrels

SEASON
All year

ROUND TRIP
3.6 km (2 ¼ miles)

TERRAIN
Flat. Forest trail and service road. Rice Lake Loop trail is suitable for wheelchairs.

FAMILY WALK
The illustrated leaflet for the Forest Ecology Loop might enhance the walk for children. There is a jetty and covered picnic table on the east shore of Rice Lake.

HERE IS AN EASY, ANYTIME WALK for the whole family—shady and cool on a hot day, short enough for a brisk winter outing, and within easy reach of the city. Please note that dogs are not allowed in the demonstration forest.

The forest stretches along the Seymour River Valley, bounded by Lynn Creek to the west and Mount Seymour to the east. A paved service road, closed to motorists but open to cyclists and in-line skaters at weekends, extends for 11 km (6 ½ miles) to Seymour Lake and dam at the forest's northern boundary. A hiking trail parallels the Seymour River to the mid-valley point, while others link up with trails in Mount Seymour Provincial Park. Coyotes, bears, cougars, bobcats and deer make their home in the forest, all of them practised at avoiding encounters with humans. Nevertheless, you should look out for deer on this walk, in brushy areas or a forest clearing.

To combine two interesting loop trails into one varied walk, start from the northeast corner of the parking lot and cross the paved road to join the I.R.M. Trail at information panel no. 6. Immediately, you step into an idyllic forest of tall, straight conifers rising from an understorey of huckleberry, ferns and salal. Conifers grew upon this earth millions of years before the appearance of broadleaf trees, shrubs, flowers and grass. Being able to retain their needle leaves throughout the year enables evergreens to stretch their growing season by making food early in spring and late into fall, essential to the trees' survival in the harsh environment of mountain or tundra. Even in winter, when the tree is dormant, the waxy needles help to prevent the loss of moisture needed to keep the roots from drying out. Often, the evergreen benefits from a relationship with certain fungi that attach themselves to the root tips and help to draw in nutrients; in return, the tree supplies the fungi with needed chemicals.

The trail swings left and continues through "managed" forest where Douglas fir and western red cedar have been planted on carefully chosen sites, interspersed with western hemlock that seeded itself. Many large stumps remain from early logging operations, as well as smaller ones from more recent thinning. After crossing a track, you enter an open, shrubby area deliberately created by clearcut logging, a temporary, light-filled oasis that provides food and cover for birds and animals, as well as a hunting ground for predators. Here you might come across a black-tailed deer browsing on twigs.

Our small black-tails are a coastal version of mule deer. They are grey-brown or buff, sometimes reddish, with a white throat patch and a mostly black tail. Deer usually feed at dawn and dusk, eating greedily while they are out in the open, soon retreating to cover where they can regurgitate the food and chew the cud in safety. They leave plenty of signs of their presence: raggedly broken twigs, black roundish droppings, wedge-shaped tracks made by their cloven hoofs. You might also notice their beds on the forest floor or, in late summer, shreds of velvet where a male has rubbed his antlers against a tree. But you will be fortunate, and cleverer than a cougar, if you spot the dappled back of a carefully hidden, sleeping fawn.

Leaving the clearing, the path enters an area of "unmanaged" forest that tells its own story. Since the last load of trees was hauled out in the 1920s, fires, storms and nature's own method of regeneration have had their way, unassisted by forest experts. Old trees lie where they fell, moss-covered, returning to the soil; seedlings sprout where they can, and flourish or die depending on the light, nourishment and space they

Rice Lake

win for themselves. Amid the seeming chaos, countless animals and insects play their part in the life of the forest.

After crossing the paved road, you descend on a wide track to Rice Lake. From the sheltered picnic table, you can turn right to include the lake trail in your walk, or left to return to the parking lot. If you choose to set off on an anticlockwise circuit of the lake, watch for the first side trail to the left, a short loop with two bridges and views across the water to the mountains of Lynn Headwaters regional park. Rejoining the main trail, you descend past a wet area choked with sedges and water lilies, then pass a road on the right before arriving at the northern tip of Rice Lake. Its odd shape, with many bays and promontories, adds a certain charm to this manmade lake, created from a marsh to supply early North Vancouver residents with water.

Next on your itinerary is the Forest Ecology Loop, an interesting side trip through three different forest sites. The illustrated leaflets usually provided at the information stand are helpful and will keep the children occupied looking for the various plants and objects described. In case this guide is not available, I mention a few things here.

In the moist, productive area through which you set off, you might

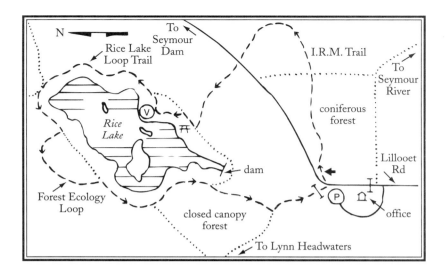

find bunchberry and false azalea beneath the firs, cedars and hemlocks. Cones are plentiful, so squirrels should be around, and flocks of tiny kinglets could be foraging for insects among the conifer branches. Next comes a long boardwalk to take you across a depression in the land. Only the cedars can tolerate the wet ground here, though hemlock seedlings may thrive on the tops of old stumps. Skunk cabbage, of course, is in its element, and frogs and newts may use the temporary ponds. As you walk on, the land rises towards a steep ridge. There are outcroppings of rock around which salal and sword fern have taken hold, and the fast-draining ground encourages Douglas firs and western white pine.

The Ecology Loop returns you to the main trail, and as you stroll along the west side of the lake enjoying glimpses of its coves and headlands, you will pass through other forest sites. You will see evergreens give way to alder, salmonberry and a flurry of foxgloves; farther on, after a left turn where the Lynn Headwaters Trail joins, a dark, closed-canopy hemlock forest takes over. Trail signs keep you on track for the forest entrance, and after walking through a final stand of alder, you step out through the yellow gate into the parking lot, having explored a few trails and had a close look at a working forest.

HOW TO GET THERE: Leave Highway 1 (the Upper Levels Highway) at the Lillooet Road exit 22. Drive north on Lillooet Road, past Capilano College, and continue on the gravel road to its end at the demonstration forest entrance. Journey time: 40 minutes.

30
First Lake, Hollyburn

WEST VANCOUVER

HIGHLIGHTS
Forest and subalpine lake; Hollyburn Lodge, Baden-Powell Trail; 1200-year-old yellow cedar; king gentians, bunchberry; gray jays

SEASON
June to November

ROUND TRIP
3.5 km (2 miles)

TERRAIN
Some climbing. Forest trail, access road, cross-country ski trails.

FAMILY WALK
Blueberry lovers may find it difficult to tear themselves away from the fruit-laden bushes around First Lake; tasty huckleberries can be found flanking the ski trails in midsummer, too.

A NETWORK OF HIKING TRAILS has existed on Hollyburn since the 1920s, interlaced today with wide cross-country ski trails that add to walking possibilities in the summer. The ridge and summit trails are beyond the scope of this book; many of the lower trails, too, include considerable climbing, putting beautiful Blue Gentian and Lost lakes beyond the reach of some walkers. First Lake, however, is easily attainable from the cross-country parking lot and has plenty of subalpine charm, as well as being the site of historic Hollyburn Lodge. The circular walk suggested, using hiking and cross-country ski trails, offers much of interest, from gentians to gray jays and bears to blueberries.

In case the mention of bears has stopped you in your tracks, please consider a few facts. Bears are everywhere in the forests and mountains around Vancouver, whether you see them or not. The wilderness is their home. You may see bear tracks or droppings on the trail or you might glimpse a bear foraging in a berry patch, in which case count yourself fortunate but leave the animal in peace. To avoid surprising a bear, talk or sing as you walk along the trail, or attach a small bell to your pack. Read a copy of the excellent leaflet "Safety Guide to Bears in the Wild" put out by the Province of B.C. Wildlife Branch, usually available outside the ranger station at First Lake.

A short distance before the signposted turning to the cross-country parking lot, a pullout on the left side of Cypress Parkway allows you to look at a 1200-year-old yellow cedar, probably one of the oldest living cedars in the world, with a diameter of 3 metres (9 ½ feet). Many remnants of old-growth forest remain on Hollyburn, providing a limited and uncertain habitat for the endangered northern spotted owl. The existence of both is in constant jeopardy from ever-expanding recreational development, as are many of the region's much-loved hiking trails. Walk on Hollyburn while you can.

Driving to the far end of the extensive cross-country parking area, you will be well placed to set off on the trail that heads south from there into the forest. In summer this delightful path is bordered by bunchberry, queen's cup, foamflower, twistedstalk and star-flowered Solomon's-seal. Mosses and beds of delicate oak fern brighten the forest floor. All too soon you step out onto a stony access road, along which you continue the short climb to First Lake by heading uphill to the left. A scattering of cabins remains beside the lake, presided over by the old red-painted Hollyburn Lodge. Built in 1926, the now dilapidated building has welcomed generations of hikers and skiers to countless events. Sadly, it may be too far gone to be restored.

Keeping the lodge on your left, you join a major trail along the lakeshore. The peaceful body of water lies nestled in its hollow, surrounded by subalpine conifers and well furnished with blueberry bushes. You have only to settle yourself at a picnic table and a rustle of wings signals the arrival of gray jays, those self-appointed guardians of picnic spots, to share your lunch. It is hard to resist the friendly birds, so willing to alight on your hand for a crumb or a piece of fruit. Their fluffy grey and white feathers are always immaculate, dark eyes bold and inquisitive. Though often silent while watching the lunch packet, gray jays can be noisy companions in the forest, following your progress with derisive whistles and chuckles or a burst of song borrowed from another bird.

Cross the dam at the south end of the lake, opposite the ranger station, and proceed to a four-way junction. A left turn onto the Wells Gray ski trail keeps you on the suggested circuit, but to look for king gentians you should venture a short distance to the right along the

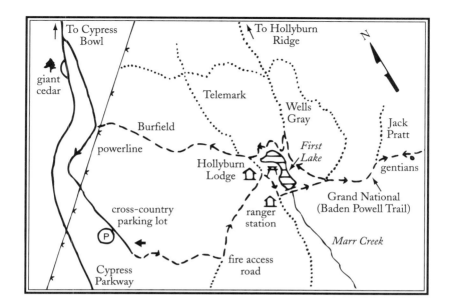

Grand National ski trail. (Ski trail signs are fastened high on tree trunks.) The gentians often bloom from July to early October, so there is plenty of opportunity to find them if you know where to look. Follow the wide Grand National, actually part of Vancouver Boy Scouts' famous Baden-Powell Trail, which extends for 41.7 km (25 miles) along the north shore mountains from Horseshoe Bay to Deep Cove. After a few minutes of walking, you will pass the Jack Pratt ski trail on the left. Now, as the track descends and becomes narrower, begin to look closely at the small, wet meadow patches on the right of the trail. This is where the gentians grow. A cabin in the trees opposite is a good landmark.

The king gentian is a sturdy perennial, growing from thick, fleshy roots, often among other bog plants such as swamp laurel, asphodel and deer cabbage. The gentian can grow to 60 cm (24 inches) or more, bearing clusters of large, deep blue flowers at the ends of leafy stalks. The oval blooms, sometimes streaked with green, are shaped somewhat like the sceptre carried by a sovereign, hence their name.

Retrace your steps to the four-way junction. A short climb up the Wells Gray ski trail brings you to a viewpoint overlooking the lake, the slopes of Black Mountain visible in the distance. A few metres ahead, take the minor, left-hand path descending towards the lake. In May and June, the beds of bunchberry along this trail will be covered with greenish-white flowers surrounded by white bracts, looking exactly like the

King gentians

miniature dogwoods they are. This beautiful little plant grows from creeping underground stems to brighten many forest trails. By August, clusters of scarlet berries, or drupes (pulpy one-seeded fruits), appear above the whorls of leaves. Bunchberry often shares its site with queen's cup, or beadlily.

The trail crosses a creek and winds between blueberry bushes and clumps of red heather, then passes a small pond full of buckbean, also decorated with showy white flowers in early summer, to join the lakeshore trail. Turn right, but instead of marching straight back to the parking lot on the wide track heading left, continue to a fork, where Burfield and Telemark ski trails go their separate ways. Burfield is your route, completing the circuit with an easy ten-minute walk through the forest, from which you emerge onto the powerline above the cross-country parking access road, a short distance west of your car.

HOW TO GET THERE: Leave Highway 1 (Upper Levels highway) in West Vancouver at the Cypress Provincial Park exit 8. Drive up Cypress Parkway for about 14 km (8 ½ miles) to parking lot 4 for the cross-country ski area. Journey time: 40 minutes.

31
Lighthouse Park

WEST VANCOUVER

HIGHLIGHTS
Virgin forest, rocky headland; lighthouse, sea views; arbutus; wild-flowers; seabirds; intertidal life

SEASON
All year

ROUND TRIP
2 km (1¼ miles)

TERRAIN
Some climbing. Access road, uneven forest trail, rough paths onto headland.

FAMILY WALK
Parties including the very young and the not-so-agile might prefer a short walk down the service road to the picnic tables near the lighthouse cairn.

THE FIRST LIGHTHOUSE ON Point Atkinson was built in 1874 to guide ships on their way to the sawmills and logging camps along Burrard Inlet. The 75 ha (185 acres) of forested Crown land north of the lighthouse was reserved as a dark backdrop for the flashing light, leaving us today with a rare pocket of virgin forest, spared from the saws. Because of the varied topography of Point Atkinson, several different types of vegetation exist: ferns and mosses on the rounded granite knolls scattered throughout the park; giant firs on the gentler slopes and valleys; cedars, maples, alders and shrubs along the streams. The white granite headlands host their own community of arbutus, shore pine, manzanita, kinnikinnick, and finally intertidal plants and animals.

This is a wilderness park with wilderness trails. On any route other than the service road, walkers must step over tree roots and around rocks. Light boots are an asset. Dry weather is safest, although I confess to having enjoyed many rainy walks in Lighthouse Park by default, when inclement weather prevented a mountain hike. The rainforest in a downpour is a wondrous place.

The valley trail suggested here is well used and easy to find. Go through the gate at the top (south end) of the parking area and walk along the service road for a few metres until you see a post numbered 2, located on the left side of the road between a labelled western hemlock and Douglas fir. Tall trees close in on you as you descend on this trail to a junction with a connecting trail from the service road. Keep left and continue the gradual descent through the groves of Douglas fir, western hemlock and western red cedar, with a typical coastal forest herb layer of sword fern, salal and Oregon grape. Huckleberry and salmonberry appear where light and moisture prevail.

Shortly after passing a trail joining from the east, watch for a labelled grand fir standing to the left of the path. Only a few old specimens exist in the park, not always easy to recognize when their distinctive sprays of flat needles, arranged in two rows along the twig, are high above one's head. The greenish seed cones too, upright on the branches as with all true firs, are high in the crown of the tree.

As you approach the coast, a minor path leads left to Starboat Cove, an inviting spot with a good view cityward, but an awkward scramble down to the driftwood-choked beach. Most people will find the headlands of East Beach easier to attain, so follow the valley trail through a patch of tall salal, past side trails to Arbutus Knoll, until you arrive among the forestry buildings at the end of the service road. Keeping Phyl Munday House on your left, walk down towards the former lightkeeper's house (Point Atkinson lighthouse became automated in 1996) where a sign "To East Beach" points left. All trails leading to the shore are marked with blue triangles, so keep a lookout for these as you walk between the buildings and down the narrow path that brings you out above the headland. From here, some routes are easier than others. Young families will have no problem scrambling down to the driftwood beach; others might adopt the method used by the smaller children— sit, slither and stretch—or cast about for the safest path onto the most easterly headland, from which there is much to be seen.

The slopes above the open rocks are clothed with arbutus, fir and stunted lodgepole pine, often referred to as shore pine. The arbutus, or madrona, is a broadleaved native evergreen, found in Canada only along the coast of southwest British Columbia. It is unmistakeable with its heavy, irregular branches and annually peeling orange-red bark. In

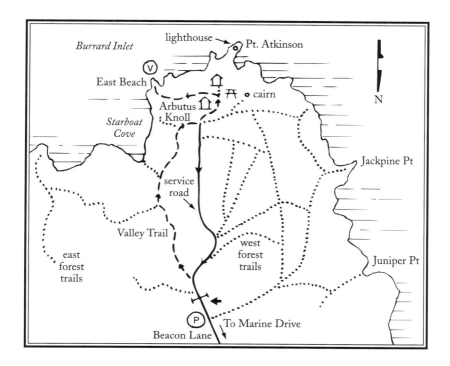

spring, drooping clusters of white bell-shaped flowers show up against the dark green leaves; red berries follow, somewhat dry and seedy, but popular with birds. You might spot the cheeky, apelike faces of yellow monkey flower peeping from shady ledges, also gumweed, a halophytic plant growing in crevices within reach of the salt spray from which it takes its nutrients—look for a plant with a leafy stem and yellow flowers whose bracts are coated with a gummy substance. There used to be exquisite chocolate lilies and blue harvest lilies on the park's headlands, but these seem less common nowadays.

If you are careful and sure-footed, you might like to explore the intertidal zones for marine life. Because the cliffs of Point Atkinson are exposed to the surf, only the most tenacious marine animals and plants are successful in clinging to the rocks. A search of tide pools and rocks above the mid-tide zone could yield shield limpets, clamped firmly to home base until the tide returns with its bounty of life-giving algae upon which to browse. Don't dislodge limpets—they cannot right themselves and will only get picked up by predators or battered by the surf. A purple starfish is always a pleasing find; look in shallow water or on rocks around barnacle and mussel beds upon which it feeds. The starfish has

neither head nor tail, but moves in any direction by means of numerous tube feet along its rays. Having straddled and prised open a bivalve with these useful appendages, the star then turns its own stomach inside out over the hapless occupant and digests it. The purple starfish (which can also be orange, yellow or brown) can also regenerate a lost ray. Because of our curiosity about these feats, we humans are probably the star's greatest enemy. Please don't let the children take one home.

If beachcombing is too hazardous for you, or turns up no interesting creatures, there is plenty to watch offshore: tugs, freighters, sailboats, gulls and diving birds, quite likely a passing harbour seal. Sometimes it's good just to doze in the sun, listen to the gulls and the waves and be buzzed occasionally by a rufous hummingbird.

Returning to the parking lot by the service road is not as dull as it might sound. The road climbs gently through the heart of the forest, past several mossy outcroppings clothed with mats of licorice fern. At a clearing on the left, a cross-section of a 525-year-old Douglas fir is displayed, its long life annotated according to its growth rings. A network of trails, some steep and rough, lace the park west of the service road, leading to Jackpine and Juniper points, the latter a prime spot to watch for shorebirds in late summer and fall—destinations for another day.

HOW TO GET THERE: From the West Vancouver end of the Lions Gate bridge, drive west on Marine Drive for 10 km (6 miles) to Beacon Lane, where a Lighthouse Park sign directs you left. Follow Beacon Lane to the parking area. Journey time: 40 minutes.

By bus: The No. 250 from Park Royal will take you to Marine Drive and Beacon Lane, from where you will have a 400 m (¼ mile) walk to the trailhead.

FACING PAGE: *Rocks at East Beach*

32
Yew Lake

CYPRESS PROVINCIAL PARK
WEST VANCOUVER

HIGHLIGHTS
Subalpine lake and meadows, old-growth forest; blueberries, white rhododendron, aquatic plants; gray jays, chickadees, flycatchers, swifts, raptors

SEASON
July to October

ROUND TRIP
1.6 km (1 mile); optional side trip to the viewpoint is an additional 1.2 km (¾ mile).

TERRAIN
Flat. Well-groomed trail, accessible to wheelchairs.

FAMILY WALK
Be sure to pull in at High View Lookout on Cypress Parkway for a panoramic view of the city and beyond. For quieter contemplation, one or two seats are provided beside Yew Lake.

AT 1000 M (3300 FEET), Cypress Bowl is a transitional region where the coastal forest of western hemlock and Douglas fir begins to give way to what is known to biologists as the Mountain Hemlock Zone.

The building of a firm gravel path through the marshy meadows surrounding Yew Lake must have been a challenge for Federation of Mountain Clubs of B.C. crews. Those for whom mountain walks are usually an impossibility can only be grateful for this labour of love, which allows the easy exploration of the subalpine lake and meadows with their distinctive plants and trees. Interpretive signs along the way add interest, as does a short additional loop trail through a stand of old-growth forest. A word of caution: the heavy snowfall at this elevation may linger until June, so make this a summer or fall outing.

The signposted Yew Lake Nature Trail begins just beyond the gate

Water lilies in Yew Lake

and ticket office to the north of the parking lot. Since you will be following the gravel path, there is no danger of getting lost, and detailed trail directions are not necessary. The walk is described here as a clockwise circuit, first following Cypress Creek to its source, then returning via the Old Growth Loop.

The creek chatters its way between banks of red heather, blueberry and huckleberry bushes. If you are able to use the trail in late spring, you will see the handsome bell-shaped flowers of the white rhododendron and the smaller pinkish blooms of copperbush. By midsummer these two shrubs appear as a thicket, and only close observation will show that the rhododendron leaves are slightly hairy and often mottled with yellow, and that the protruding pistils of the copperbush flowers are still visible after the petals have faded.

Some members of the lily family grow beside the trail. You could hardly miss the exotic-looking false hellebore, with its large, deeply ribbed leaves and droopy tassels of tiny, yellow-green flowers. Less noticeable in the profusion of greenery is twistedstalk, a kinky, oddly structured plant whose translucent, oblong red berries might catch your eye on an August or September walk.

The familiar western hemlocks of lower elevations have given way to the subalpine mountain hemlock, a smaller, scrubbier tree with disorderly leaves bristling around the twig and a larger, more cylindrical cone than that of western hemlock. Western white pine is easily identified by its silvery-grey bark and bundles of five long needles. The mature cones are long and slender, often slightly curved. The beautiful amabilis fir is found here too, its lower branches sweeping to the ground. White lines on the underside of the needle leaves give this fir its silvery appearance. As with all true firs, the purplish cones are erect on the twig. Don't look for yew trees—there are none at Yew Lake!

With the outlet creek now on your left, you will come to a pool fringed with deer cabbage, a semiaquatic plant described on an interpretive panel. In due course the path opens out to the lakeshore, from where you can gaze across the beds of buckbean and water lilies to the forested slope of Black Mountain. This is a good place to watch for birds. As well as the ubiquitous gray jays, who know what picnic tables are for, you might see warblers, flycatchers, the chestnut-backed chickadee, the hermit thrush, Steller's jays, and the little Vaux's swift twinkling and gliding over water. Often mistaken for swallows, swifts are in fact akin to hummingbirds and share with them long, narrow wings and tiny feet.

The path follows the shore until the end of the lake is in sight, when it heads off northward, winding its way through fragile meadows of sedges and small pools. Shortly after passing a panel describing the glacial erratics that can be seen to the right of the trail, you head left (straight ahead is your return route to the parking lot) into a surprising

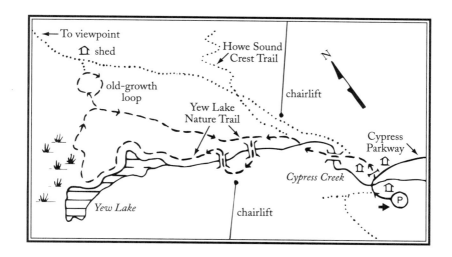

remnant of old-growth forest. The majestic western hemlocks tower above you as you walk the short loop trail.

For a longer walk (this route is not smooth enough for wheelchairs), you can take the path between the two large trees on the north side of the forest to emerge onto a logging road opposite a small building. A short walk westward brings you to a viewpoint overlooking Bowen Island across Howe Sound. You may spot hawks soaring over this open burn area. The Northern harrier, the red-tailed hawk and the American kestrel are some that could be seen here during the raptor migration in August and September.

Returning from the viewpoint, you can of course complete the old-growth loop and the Yew Lake circuit. But if you wish, you may return to the parking area by staying on the logging road, which, although stony underfoot, is fringed with roadside flowers such as fireweed, asters and pearly everlasting.

HOW TO GET THERE: Cypress Provincial Park is reached from Highway 1 (Upper Levels Highway) in West Vancouver by taking Cypress Bowl exit 8 and driving Cypress Parkway to its end at the downhill ski area. Journey time: 40 minutes.

33
Killarney Creek Trails

CRIPPEN REGIONAL PARK
BOWEN ISLAND

HIGHLIGHTS
Forest, lake, meadow; Snug Cove, Deep Bay lagoon, fish ladder; western red cedars; waterfowl, kingfishers

SEASON
All year

ROUND TRIP
4.5 km (2 ¾ miles)

TERRAIN
Mostly flat. Forest and meadow trails, road.

FAMILY WALK
There is an interesting boardwalk promenade fronting Snug Cove, leading to extensive picnic grounds and a trail to Dorman Point. There are some picnic tables at Killarney Lake as well.

MOST OF US ARE SUSCEPTIBLE to the magic of islands, needing only the shortest of voyages to awaken the explorer in us. Bowen Island, a mere twenty-minute ferry ride from West Vancouver, has been beguiling visitors for hundreds of years. First came the Squamish people to hunt and fish in the summer, building a smokehouse and dwellings in what is now Snug Cove. Inevitably they were followed by explorers, settlers, miners and loggers. In the early 1900s a new era in island history began when Captain John Cates, and later the Union Steamship Company, regularly ferried thousands of pleasure-seekers to disport themselves in the tearooms, dance pavilions, hotels and picnic grounds of Snug Cove. Today Bowen is a quieter place, dedicated to preserving its island environment. While the welcome is still warm, and visitors may stroll through the craft shops and partake of home baking in the restaurants, most are there to explore the parks and beaches and surrender to the island tempo.

Canada geese

Lying close to the mainland, in Howe Sound, Bowen shares our topography and weather rather than the drier climate of the other Gulf Islands. The forested slopes of Mount Gardner dominate the 10-km (6-mile)–long island, laced with old logging roads that now serve as a network of hiking trails. Within easy reach of Snug Cove, Crippen Regional Park offers less strenuous walking through forest and meadow and around Killarney Lake. These low-level trails are accessible throughout the year, and are especially attractive in fall when the leaves are turning colour. Wildlife on the island includes deer and mink, grouse, eagles, waterfowl, seabirds and fish.

Disembarking from the ferry, walk up Government Street into the centre of Snug Cove, where the Union Steamship Company Store is your starting point for today's island ramble. Leaflets on Crippen Regional Park are usually available at the information stand outside the store. Walk a few metres north along Gardena Drive to pick up Alder Grove Trail, heading into the woods on the left and signposted to Killarney Lake. Almost immediately, a worthwhile side trip presents itself, a path to the right leading through the Memorial Gardens to a rocky bluff overlooking Deep Bay and across Howe Sound to the mountains on the mainland.

Back on route, you climb gently through woodland with many old broadleaf maples and a fine mix of native plants and garden escapes along the trail, to the next wayside attraction, a platform above Killarney Creek, from where you look down through the trees to an old fish ladder. A little farther ahead, you can descend beside the falls if you wish.

Next comes Miller Road, with Hatchery Trail entering the woods opposite. As this path plunges deeper into the forest, deciduous trees give way to western red cedars, towering above carpets of sword fern. Just after crossing a bridge, you come upon two huge cedar snags on the right of the trail, the nearest one a fire-blackened shell. To stand inside this ghostly chamber is to feel the majesty of the once magnificent tree. The second snag has an interesting hole, just too high to peep inside. Closely flanked by their living neighbours, the snags resemble the ramparts of a ruined castle.

Aboriginal people believe the cedar to have spiritual power. Over thousands of years, it has been revered and used for life-sustaining purposes such as shelter, clothing, canoes, tools and medicine, as well as totem poles. Long strips of bark can be peeled off and dried for making into mats and blankets; split root-ends used for rope-making and the construction of fish traps; dugout canoes carved from cedar logs. Easily split and resistant to decay for a hundred years, cedar wood is also used today for shakes and shingles. Standing in a hushed glade at the buttressed base of a giant cedar, it is not too hard to believe that one might receive strength from the "tree of life."

After descending to a bridge over Terminal Creek, you pass through a stand of alder to join Meadow Trail. Turn right, past the equestrian ring, to cross the inviting open meadow, lush with grass and flowers in

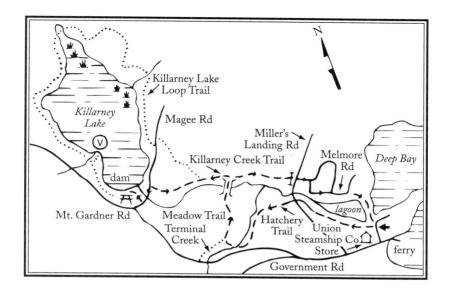

summer. I once came upon a snake sunning itself on the path here and was surprised that it had none of the yellow stripes and red markings of our northwestern garter snakes. This snake was grey with black spots— a dull fellow in appearance, but lively in manner and indignant at being disturbed. Later research indicated that this might have been a wandering garter snake, a species that is plentiful on the island. None of our garter snakes is poisonous, and all bear living young, an adaptation found only in reptiles inhabiting cool climates.

At the end of the meadow, Killarney Creek slips through its marshy surroundings, shrouded by shrubs and skunk cabbage. After crossing the bridge, turn left on Killarney Creek Trail. Cedars, maples and spruce dominate the forest here, with many ferny glades and patches of Oregon grape on higher ground. Keep left at the next fork, and after passing a group of four big maples joined at the base, you will step out onto a gravel road. Go left along it for a few metres, then right on the narrow path beside the dam to the lakeshore, where picnic tables are set beneath the trees. From here you can gaze down the lake to the drowned trees at its northern end, and enjoy the company of ducks and families of picnic-wise Canada geese at most seasons.

A 4-km (2½-mile) trail encircles the lake, crossing the marshy northern end on a boardwalk and returning along the steeper, more rugged eastern side of the lake. As a reward for strolling a little way along the lake trail you might catch the sudden flash of blue as a belted kingfisher dives from an overhanging limb and belly-flops into the water with a loud splash. The accomplished fisher then carries its prize back to the perch, whacks the fish against a branch, tosses it into the air and swallows it headfirst, fins and bones to be regurgitated later as pellets. In spite of its brash demeanour, harsh rattling voice and unkempt topknot, the kingfisher is a shy bird with secretive habits. Its nest is a deep burrow in an earth bank, excavated by both male and female until they have a tunnel up to 2 metres (6 ½ feet) in length, at the end of which a domed chamber is hollowed out for the nest.

To return to Snug Cove, retrace your steps as far as the junction with Meadow Trail, but from there carry on along Killarney Creek Trail to its end at a yellow gate on Miller's Landing Road. This final stretch is notable for many large evergreens and interesting nurse stumps. From the gate you may walk right along the road to connect with your outward route above the falls, or, for an interesting variation, cross Miller's Landing Road and set off along the road more or less opposite the yellow gate. Next, turn right on Melmore Road. Shortly after passing Lenora Road on your left, watch for a track heading downhill to the right, just after a bend. This trail may not be signposted, but leads you in a few minutes to a causeway between the lagoon and Deep Bay.

The banks of the lagoon are shrubby with willows and sweet gale, brightened in fall by patches of purple asters. Ducks paddle contentedly in the weedy, still water, sifting the surface for anything edible, occasionally snapping a wet bill at a passing dragonfly. On the seaward side, Killarney Creek spills out beneath the causeway, and gulls wheel over the sheltered bay or doze and preen on the beach. Walkers with time to spare before the next ferry may be tempted to doze on the beach too, but remember it is a five-minute walk up Gardena Drive to the Union Steamship Company Store and a five-minute trot down Government Street to the ferry slip.

HOW TO GET THERE: Take Highway 1 to Horseshoe Bay in West Vancouver and leave the car in the ferry terminal parking lot. Journey time: 45 minutes (allow time for parking and purchasing ferry tickets). By bus: No. 250 and 257 from Park Royal go to Horseshoe Bay.

Ferries to Bowen Island run almost hourly. Phone B.C. Ferries Corporation at 669-1211 for sailing times.

34
Porteau Cove

HIGHLIGHTS
Beach; Howe Sound views, the *Royal Hudson*, scuba divers; intertidal life

SEASON
All year

ROUND TRIP
Up to 1.6 km (1 mile)

TERRAIN
One short climb. Road, trail and pebble beach.

FAMILY WALK
Most children are accomplished beachcombers and will be happy here for hours. Descending and emerging scuba divers add interest too.

HOWE SOUND, BRITISH COLUMBIA'S most southerly fjord and a legacy from the last glacial period, stretches for 44 km (26 miles) from Horseshoe Bay to Squamish. Along its length, the sound receives the waters of numerous creeks that rush headlong down the sheer mountainsides, torrents that call for resourceful engineering and constant maintenance to keep the winding highway and railroad tracks safe for traffic. The drive from Horseshoe Bay is spectacular, with views across the water to Bowen, Gambier and Anvil islands and the mountains of the Sunshine Coast beyond. However, there are few places along the sound where one can explore on foot without undertaking a rugged hike. So whether you are en route to Squamish or Whistler, or simply enjoying a drive up the sound, a break at Porteau Cove, with its easy access to the water, can be very welcome.

The park is a 4½-ha (11-acre) strip comprising mixed forest, broad beaches and a rocky headland. As well as a boat launch, a jetty and a number of picnic tables around the parking lot, there are fifty to sixty campsites strung out among the trees above the beach. The bay is popular with divers, and to enhance underwater exploration several vessels have been sunk offshore to provide a base for marine life. The park's well-kept secret, however, is that the real Porteau Cove is tucked away out of sight of the busy parking area, and to visit it you must take a walk.

Set off along the paved road that runs beside the railway, following signs to the walk-in campsites. From Wednesday to Sunday in the summer, a train whistle and puffs of steam herald the approach of Vancouver's famous vintage steam train, the *Royal Hudson*, on its regular sightseeing run between North Vancouver and Squamish. It is customary to wave—who could resist anyway? The road is pleasant to walk along, bordered in summer by a tumble of wildflowers beneath hedges of oceanspray and roses, opening out beyond the last campsites into a lawn shaded by several fine old Sitka spruce. This area, with its walled lagoon and ornamental trees, was once the site of a small settlement built by a sand and gravel company in the early 1900s. Today, the gardens boast an amphitheatre for visitors and a new footbridge across the lagoon.

The cove, sheltered by an enclosing headland, offers some interesting beachcombing among the ancient driftwood, some of which is encrusted with acorn barnacles. We tend not to cast a second look at these familiar crustaceans, but in fact the barnacle's life is intriguing. Lying on its back inside the miniature volcano, the animal reaches out with its legs to catch plankton when the waves wash over it. At low tide, it seals itself off behind a hinged cover for protection. Barnacle larvae swim out adventurously from the family home, only in middle age settling down to a sedentary life in the high tide zone.

Depending on the tide, and whether you are able to keep your footing on the slippery rockweed, you will find beds of blue mussels around the water's edge, probably attracting hungry seabirds, crows and even starlings. Mussels are bivalves like clams and oysters, but they attach themselves by secreted threads at their pointed ends, the dense masses of mussels often harbouring unseen colonies of worms and snails. Inside its elegant home, the mussel lives upside down, head near the point of attachment, and lives by waving tiny hairs to draw in plankton and oxygen from the water.

Diligent searchers might find red rock crabs, hermit crabs and checkered periwinkles, while rockhounds will be pleased with the colourful and varied pebbles underfoot. It is always rewarding to poke about in the strand, that is, the line of debris deposited by the tide at the high water mark. Among the weeds and driftwood are shells, bits and pieces of crabs, skeletons, and sometimes treasures from foreign shores.

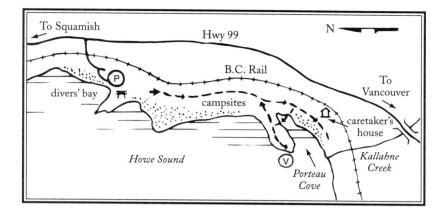

As you disturb the jetsam, you will certainly wake up the sandhoppers that live beneath it in burrows, from which they venture forth for night-time raids on the strand.

Our Pacific waters support an abundance of marine algae, including the world's largest kelp beds. As well as the brown and yellow rockweed, or popping wrack, with its inflated tips, you might find washed-up pieces of bright green sea lettuce or ragged brown blades of kelp. Instead of roots, most algae have a "holdfast," either fibrous or disklike, with which to attach themselves to a rock or pebble, and some have floats to hold themselves up to the surface for light. Although we do not use our seaweeds as much commercially as do some countries, these plants provide food, shelter and oxygen for intertidal and subtidal animals.

If you have wandered far in your search for marine life, you might prefer to return to the lagoon by the service road that runs behind the big firs and maples overlooking the beach. This is the access road to the caretaker's house—please respect his private property. Next, head across the footbridge to pick up the trail to the lookout platform on the headland. The short climb is eased by a wooden staircase with railings and takes you through Douglas firs and cedars, arbutus and shore pine, to a fine viewpoint overlooking Howe Sound. An information panel names some of the birds that frequent the bay. In spring and summer these might include loons, oystercatchers and marbled murrelets.

Having read that rare twayblade orchids grow on the lookout hill, I once followed a side trail in the hope of finding some. In a few metres, I came to a clearing in which lay a log used by squirrels as a feeding site, cone scales and other debris piled high upon it. Within moments a Douglas squirrel appeared bearing a fresh cone. This was quickly

Driftwood

cached, away from my prying eyes, and the harvester scampered off for more. I didn't find any twayblades, but there was a patch of rattlesnake plantains growing out of the moss in the clearing, their spikes of greenish flowers rising from a rosette of dark green leaves, mottled and striped with white. Some coastal peoples used the rattlesnake plantain orchid as a good luck charm. I considered it a lucky find as the plant does not flower every year but only when conditions are favourable, and I returned to the main trail well satisfied.

Having made your way back to the parking lot by the road or the beach, you can watch wet-suited divers emerging from the depths or share a snack with the resident white-crowned sparrows patrolling the picnic tables.

HOW TO GET THERE: The park is situated on Howe Sound 24 km (15 miles) north of Horseshoe Bay. Take Highway 99 north. Journey time: 50 minutes.

35
Brackendale Dykes

BRACKENDALE

HIGHLIGHTS
Squamish River, mountain views; bald eagles, Barrow's goldeneye; harbour seals

SEASON
Mid-November to mid-February for eagles

ROUND TRIP
Up to 1 km (½ mile)

TERRAIN
Flat. Gravel dyke-top accessible to wheelchairs.

FAMILY WALK
A winter visit to Shannon Falls could be included in this outing—the ice formations can be spectacular.

DURING THE WINTER months the Cheekye, Cheakamus, Mamquam and Squamish rivers deposit a harvest of decaying, spawned-out salmon along the banks and gravel bars. Aware of this annual feast, thousands of bald eagles from all over western North America congregate in the lower Squamish valley, and other winter feeding grounds, to feast on the carcasses. More than 3500 birds were counted around Squamish in 1994—one of the largest concentration of eagles in the world. This great gathering of raptors is an unforgettable sight, well worth the drive from Vancouver and the likelihood of facing the "Squamish," the arctic wind that sweeps in rude gusts down the Squamish valley from the northern mountains. Try to choose one of those spells of benign weather that bless our west-coast winters and enjoy the bonus of the snow-capped Garibaldi massif and Tantalus mountains sparkling in the sun.

A word of warning: recent studies indicate that the number of visitors, especially at weekends, is disturbing the eagles and driving them to the more remote west side of the river. Although people are welcome to walk on the dykes, certain traditional eagle-viewing areas are at present being considered out of bounds, and volunteer wardens may be abroad, directing and advising human traffic. Also, visitors are being encouraged to view the eagles from rafts and canoes, as this is thought to be less threatening to the birds, and a number of organizations run tours for this purpose. If this does not appeal to you, perhaps a discreet midweek visit would be most satisfactory; go quietly, don't venture onto the gravel bars or try to get too close to the birds, and raise camera and binoculars slowly.

The stretch of the Government Road dyke known as Eagle Run extends for about 400 m (¼ mile) around the mouth of Dryden Creek, giving a view across the river to a gravel beach backed by cottonwoods, above which the mountainside rises steeply. Walking northward past a small mobile home site, you will come to a wide bend in the river, around which the opaquely green water swings quite fiercely, leaving a strand of driftwood on the far shore. The dyke continues beside a slough fringed with alders, eventually curving to the left and ending at private property. Across the slough, a wide gravel beach with patches of vegetation is a good place to observe eagles, gulls and diving birds partaking of the feast.

Adult bald eagles are dark brown with white heads, necks and tails. Juveniles, at first uniformly dark then later becoming blotched with white, take four to five years to mature. Your binoculars will show you that the eagle's bill is a strong, yellow hook, designed for tearing flesh from bones. The wingspan of an eagle can be around 200 cm (7 feet) and you might feel the beat of those wings overhead as the raptor patrols the shoreline for dead fish. Primarily a scavenger, the bald eagle is able to store about two pounds of food in its crop, against days when the pickings are slim.

Walking southward along the dyke, you will have a good view of eagles perched on the cottonwoods across the river. With binoculars you may be able to observe the eagle hierarchy: adult females, always the largest birds, take the highest branches, with the smaller males and juveniles in descending order below. As you approach a yellow gate across the dyke, you will notice a bay or channel opposite, where many birds may be congregated around the shallow water. Downstream lies a treed island, an immense jumble of logs caught on its northern shore.

Although Eagle Run provides limited walking, the river's passing parade holds your attention for as long as you want to stay outdoors. It is quite likely that the round, dark head of a seal or sea lion will break

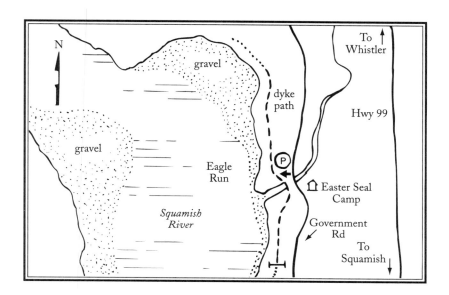

the surface of the water, or a wheeling, tumbling flock of crows catch your eye. Scan the river, too, for Barrow's goldeneye ducks bobbing along, sometimes sideways or even backwards in the strong current. The dapper black-and-white males have dark, purplish heads rising abruptly from a stubby bill. The white crescent at the base of the bill distinguishes the Barrow's from the common goldeneye, which sports a circular white patch. The females of both species are brown-headed and elsewhere soberly attired in grey.

The scene looks timeless and peaceful—the mountains and forests opposite, the birds feeding on the gravel bars, the green river rushing by, but in fact the eagles' habitat is threatened by logging and industrial development, as well as a proposed airport for Brackendale, and the Squamish Estuary Conservation Society is pressing for at least 1000 ha (2500 acres) on the west side of the Squamish River to be reserved as a bald eagle sanctuary.

HOW TO GET THERE: Drive 8 km (5 miles) north of Squamish on Highway 99. Turn left (west) on Garibaldi Way, then right on Government Road. Park on the road opposite the Easter Seal Camp, where a sign "Eagle View" indicates access to the dyke. Journey time: 1¼ hours.

Acknowledgements

This book had its beginnings when I was a child, taught to appreciate nature by parents who loved and enjoyed the countryside. Many of us were given that early gift, or have since discovered for ourselves the lifelong pleasure that comes from observing and trying to understand the natural world. To those whose interest was never awakened, or has become dulled from lack of use, I say it is never too late to develop an acquaintance with nature and share in the joy.

Many people have had a hand in the making of this book. Park naturalists and planners have supplied material and patiently answered countless questions; local natural history societies have also been most willing to supply information and offer suggestions. Hiking friends have curbed their normal pace to lend extra pairs of eyes on nature walks.

In particular, I thank Jean Molson for accompanying me rain or shine; Susan Rowe-Evans for contributing her expert knowledge and acute observation on several walks; Veronica Shelford for getting me started with a computer and being on hand thereafter to sort out the muddles; and Norman Cousins for taking photographs of difficult subjects, often under daunting conditions. I am grateful also to Vi Wall and Jean Molson for loaning their splendid photographs.

Finally, I greatly appreciate the assistance of Dick Cannings in reviewing the manuscript and offering suggestions and advice.

I offer the result of these combined efforts as an invitation to all shades of walkers to add a new dimension to their excursions out of doors. What you make of the walks is up to you. In the end, the nature walker finds his or her own way to the first spring trillium, the bushtit's nest, the cedar grove bathed in sunlight.